ROSE SHAPIRO was born in Lo[n]... for the National Abortion Campaign, the Pregnancy Advisory Service and the Family Planning Association as organiser, counsellor and press officer respectively. Since 1980 she has worked as a freelance journalist and has written widely on matters of sexual politics, health and contraception for *City Limits, Good Housekeeping, Spare Rib, New Society, Time Out* and *Nursing Times* among other publications. She has also contributed to *Good Housekeeping Family Medical Guide*. She lives in London.

In *Contraception: A Practical and Political Guide* Rose Shapiro puts birth control into its historical, political and social context. The first part of the book covers the history and background of the contraception movement from Marie Stopes to current abortion legislation, describes battles fought on sexuality and reproductive rights for young women, and analyses the political implications behind giving and withholding information. The second part is a practical and detailed guide to all the methods of contraception available today, listing products by name, explaining exactly what is in them, how to use them and how reliable they are. This much-needed book will allow women to make a truly informed judgement on all aspects of contraception.

Contraception

A practical and political guide

Rose Shapiro

Published by VIRAGO PRESS Limited 1987
41 William IV Street, London WC2N 4DB

British Library Cataloguing in Publication Data

SHAPIRO, Rose
    Contraception : a practical and political
    guide.
    1. Contraception
    I. Title
    613.9'4   RG136

    ISBN 0-86068-657-4

Illustrations by Maggie Raynor

Photoset in North Wales by
Derek Doyle & Associates, Mold, Clwyd
Printed in Great Britain by
Cox & Wyman Ltd of Reading, Berkshire

CONTENTS

ACKNOWLEDGEMENTS

I would like to thank all those who helped when I was researching this book, including Kaye Wellings, Helen Martins, John Guillebaud, Joanna Chambers and Dilys Cossey. Thanks also to Jill Nicholls, who suggested I write it in the first place, as well as to Jean Shapiro, Angela Phillips, Sam Organ and Simon Jennings who have all helped a great deal with both ideas and encouragement. I benefitted enormously too from the knowledge and generosity of Toni Belfield, whose suggestions and comments on Part Two of the book were invaluable.

INTRODUCTION

This book is about women's health, sexuality, reproduction and history. It is based on the belief that fertility control is a political issue, and that contraception cannot be looked at without taking into account its historical and political context.

The chapters in Part One – on the history of the birth control movement, current battles about sexuality and reproduction, and the politics of information – are intended to be as much a practical resource for women using contraception as the sections in Part Two, detailing specific methods of contraception, sterilisation and abortion. The history of contraception and the birth control movement can help us understand what's behind current provision – why, for instance, doctors are in control of contraceptive prescription, why the pill has become the most widely used method of contraception, why barrier methods like the cap and diaphragm are increasingly less popular with women, and what attitudes shape research into new methods of birth control. How far are our attitudes to our sexuality influenced by others' views of what it should be, and what difference does this make to a decision about contraception? What are we prepared to do to our bodies in order to avoid conception? How much do we need to know before we choose a contraceptive method? And what difference will AIDS make to both our sexual lives and to our contraceptive choice – will we use condoms as well as our previous methods or instead of them?

There is still a great deal that is yet to be understood about current contraceptive methods. No one understands exactly how the IUD works; and there are no definite conclusions about the effect contraceptives may have on our health. Many of us feel that a

1

decision about contraception means only that we choose the best of a bad lot. Part Two of this book gives you up-to-date information about all birth control methods, including sterilisation and abortion, detailing the advantages and disadvantages of each.

Information about contraception is never value-free. The information here is intended to be a resource for women who desire to have control over their own fertility. It is written from the point of view of a consumer, not a prescriber.

1

THE EARLY
BIRTH CONTROLLERS

Where do they come from ...
what do they want?

The development of contraceptive services, both the methods
themselves and their means of distribution, has happened
remarkably quickly. A century ago the medical establishment
seemed immovably opposed to any kind of birth control. The
powerful Christian church was against any conscious attempt to
limit family size, since it believed sex to be primarily for the sake of
procreation, and the state's position reflected the religious view.

Until the last century the only reliable means of birth control
were abstinence from sex or illegal abortion. For most women the
only sources of information and help on these matters were their
women friends, neighbours and relations. But histories of
contraception show that women did try to stop pregnancy by
various mechanical methods before there was any kind of birth
control movement to tell them how to do it. Absorbent sponges,
maybe dipped in quinine, olive oil or some other substance that the
user hoped was spermicidal, were used. By the middle of the last
century devices similar to cervical caps and IUDs had been
developed, but these were often unreliable and even dangerous, and
weren't generally available. The only contraceptive that offered safe
and reliable protection from pregnancy was the condom. There are
descriptions of the condom written as long ago as the sixteenth
century, when it was made out of sheep intestines. By the end of the
nineteenth century the rubber condom was being manufactured and

widely advertised for use as a contraceptive and protective against sexually transmitted disease.

The beginnings of the birth control debate

The first public debate on contraception came with the re-publication in 1877 of a pamphlet *The Fruits of Philosophy* which advocated deliberate family limitation and the use of withdrawal or a syringe as methods of contraception. The pamphlet, written by an American doctor Charles Knowlton, had been around for forty years, and was based on the writings of Malthus, a late eighteenth-century clergyman. He was the first 'populationist', who saw population growth as leading to economic crisis as more and more people drained the world of its finite resources. He advocated celibacy and delayed marriage as the solution, but the pamphlet's writer saw these measures as inadequate and promoted contraception instead.

The publishers of the *Fruits of Philosophy* were women's rights campaigner Annie Besant and Charles Bradlaugh, MP and freethinker. There had already been a successful prosecution under the Obscene Publications Act of a bookseller who sold the pamphlet, and the Besant/Bradlaugh publication was designed to trigger public debate and to attract prosecution once more. Bradlaugh sent a copy to the police and the two were arrested and came to trial in 1877. The case got national press coverage and the defendants received considerable public support. Besant, Bradlaugh and their defence witnesses used the opportunity of the trial to publicise the need for birth control for the poor and deprived as a way of creating a more just and economically stable society. They were finally acquitted on a legal technicality.

The trial led to the formation of the Malthusian League, which propagandised population control as the answer to poverty. At first the league tried to promote birth control methods amongst the working class, but soon switched to producing propaganda for doctors and politicians. In the early 1900s the league returned to more practical publicity work, with public meetings and contraceptive demonstrations in working-class areas of London. By this time the diaphragm had been invented by a German doctor, and in 1882 the world's first contraceptive clinic had been opened in Amsterdam.

Survival of the unfittest

Malthus-inspired populationism came at the same time as the creation of a new philosophy which became popular among the British establishment and upper class. Following work on the origins of the human species there arose the idea that not only were some racial groups superior to others, but a hereditary hierarchy existed within the 'British race' itself, with some sections of it born 'racially pure' – physically and mentally superior to others of the same race. The evidence for this belief seemed obvious to its supporters. Working-class people tended to be small, unhealthy and to die younger than the middle and upper class, which was not surprising given the lack of nutrition, bad housing and health care the mass of the population faced. The working classes were also thought to be weak-willed, unintelligent and morally degenerate.

What frightened the 'superior' upper classes was the fact that the birth rate of the working class was higher than their own. Just as modern racism is fuelled by the notion of being 'swamped' by an alien invasion, this kind of eugenic prejudice was based on the fear that the apparently ever-increasing numbers of the lower classes would swamp those at the top. They believed an improvement in the living conditions of the lower classes, paid for by taxing the wealthier and, by this time, resentful sections of the population, was interfering with the 'natural selection' and 'survival of the fittest' which had controlled numbers in the past. The weak were now being allowed to live and to reproduce in a way they had not done before.

Worse still, was that from about the time of the Besant/Bradlaugh trial, middle- and upper-class Britons had been consciously limiting family size, and had been able to obtain condoms, caps and spermicides. The fear was that their numbers would reduce still further. There was also the widely held belief that the lower classes were actually more fertile, and certainly more likely (because of moral weakness) to indulge their baser and less civilised sexuality and produce more children as a result. So civilised society was becoming not only the minority, but was thought to be at risk of being wiped out altogether. Some practical intervention would have to be made where 'natural selection' had ruled in the past, if the good and the strong were to survive.

This was accompanied by the belief that anti-social behaviour (like crime and alcoholism), mental illness and physical weakness were hereditary. Anti-social individuals could only reproduce themselves, and therefore multiply the numbers of criminals, alcoholics, and other impure strains of humanity. The answer was to stop these sections of society from breeding, and to encourage the pure and strong to increase their numbers through reproduction.

Scientist Francis Galton took up the study of heredity towards the end of the nineteenth century. By this time the new science was called 'eugenics', and was interpreted to be a scientific justification for forced sterilisation of criminals, tramps and the 'mentally deficient' as well as for the encouragement of reproduction by those who were supposedly 'racially pure'. Galton preferred to pursue the latter approach, wanting those of good genetic stock to be given eugenic certificates and be urged to reproduce themselves. His belief in the idea of 'racial progress' inspired the setting up, in 1908, of the Eugenics Society. The society was not directly involved in promoting birth control, but its ideas were the inspiration for many of those who did. Galton died in 1911, having established eugenics as a 'science' which was beginning to be accepted by the medical profession. It would not be seriously questioned for many decades, when the implications of a commitment to racial purity were made so horrifyingly clear by Hitler and the Nazi movement in the years that followed. But in the early 1900s the eugenic approach was politically acceptable to both left and right in Britain.

Marie Stopes and 'Constructive Birth Control'

The suffrage campaigns for votes for women and female emancipation were not directly involved in either the Malthusian League or the Eugenics Society, but many suffrage workers were concerned with women's health and the physical welfare of mothers and children. Some of these women were also members of the Malthusian League and went on to campaign for birth control once they had secured the vote.

Attitudes to contraception were also changed by the First World War. There was widespread fear about sexually transmitted diseases, and soldiers were issued with condoms as protection from disease and to reduce the number of illegitimate children they might father. The employment of women workers at home during the war also created more support for the cause of female emancipation. Feminists were calling for a redefinition of the woman's role, and rejecting the male-determined role of woman as wife and mother. Women had seen the young sons they loved cut down in their thousands in the Great War, and would react against any encouragement to produce children who could be yet more cannon fodder. By the beginning of the 1920s the time was right for a new campaign for contraceptive provision, which would incorporate arguments for female emancipation, eugenic purity, and the relief of poverty.

The mixture of feminism, eugenics and class prejudice manifested itself in varying degrees in the work of Marie Stopes. Following the annulment of a disastrous marriage, Stopes wrote a book about sex that she hoped would save others from the same sort of miserable experience. *Married Love* was published in 1918, and stunned the British public with its explicit language and assertion of women's rights to sexual expression and enjoyment. The book was an enormous success, selling 2,000 copies within two weeks. Stopes had a scientific background, and justified much of her argument in scientific terms – she said the absorption of semen by women and vaginal secretions by men was essential to health, for instance.

Marie Stopes' biographer, Ruth Hall, has pointed out that much of *Married Love* was based on the ideas of others already writing about sexuality: Edward Carpenter, Olive Schreiner and Havelock Ellis. To these ideas Stopes added a political belief that society itself could be transformed if people were sexually fulfilled within the mystical union of marriage. The perfect marriage would make each partner 'a fitter and more perfect instrument for one's own particular work, the results of which should be shared by society as a whole', she wrote.

Stopes had met American birth control campaigner Margaret Sanger some years before, and she was committed to the use of birth control, especially for the poor and deprived. Later in 1918 Stopes wrote *Wise Parenthood* which gave detailed descriptions of contraceptive methods. In 1921 she opened the Mothers' Clinic for Constructive Birth Control (known as CBC) in Holloway, north London. This was Britain's first birth control clinic, and it provided women with cervical caps to be used with an oil-based dissolving pessary containing quinine.

Over the years Marie Stopes has become almost sanctified as a progressive pioneer of women's control of their fertility. But although she had many progressive attitudes about women's sexuality and the need to dispel ignorance, 'anyone short of an extreme reactionary would today regard some of her ideas with horror' as Ruth Hall puts it. Stopes' promotion of birth control was to a great extent her second-best resort – what she would have preferred to see was 'the sterilisation of those totally unfit for parenthood made an immediate possibility, indeed made compulsory'. This would enable the race to '... rapidly quell the stream of depraved, hopeless and wretched lives which are at present ever increasing in proportion in our midst'. Here once more are the ideas of the eugenicists and Malthusians, where the purity and strength of the race are seen to be put at risk by the unchecked reproduction of the lower classes. Horror of 'inferior stock' and the 'racially negligent' spurred her on in her work at the clinic, with its letterhead motto 'Joyous and Deliberate Motherhood. A Sure Light in Our Racial Darkness', and where working-class women were provided with the 'Pro-Race' brand of contraceptives.

As well as the risk of racial impurity Marie Stopes saw greater and immediate danger in the increasing numbers of the working class. The Russian Revolution of 1917 had shaken the ruling classes of the rest of the world, who were terrified that they too risked the same fate. It was the working class who had been behind this revolution, and by allowing them to multiply at such a rate 'we have been breeding revolutionaries', Stopes wrote in her book *Radiant Motherhood*, published in 1920. Two years later, writing in *Birth Control News*, she developed this idea still further. 'The root of revolution is not obvious,' she wrote, 'it is hidden in the most secret place – in the womb of woman when she bears children warped by disease, or warped by her hatred and revolt against involuntary motherhood.'

But even these ideas did not sway the religious and medical opposition to contraception, which they thought encouraged immorality and disease. The medical establishment was particularly opposed to Stopes' view that doctors weren't needed to provide birth control – she preferred to employ nurses and midwives at her clinic, and she herself had no medical qualifications.

By the beginning of the 1920s the Malthusian League, prompted by Marie Stopes' publicity success, was once again interested in practical provision of contraception for the poor, rather than propagandising populationist views amongst the middle and upper class. The Walworth Women's Welfare Centre ran mother and baby clinics, as well as providing the diaphragm (which they called the Dutch cap because it had first been used in Holland) and the condom to those who were brave enough to attend. Clinic workers were pelted with stones, apples and eggs, with women clients being verbally harangued as they entered. And although public attention continued to be focused on the issue of birth control, few women actually used the clinics. Those who wanted contraception would instead get it from private gynaecologists, on mail-order, or buy it from high-street 'rubber shops'. In 1922 the Malthusian League gave up running the Walworth clinic and passed it over to a committee which in 1924 became the Society for the Provision of Birth Control Clinics (see page 11).

Apart from having to cope with the wrath of the anti-contraception establishment, the birth controllers were by now fighting amongst themselves. Marie Stopes styled herself as the true and only pioneer in the field and was angry about the setting up of the Walworth clinic, believing the Malthusian League had stolen her idea. There was also considerable dispute about the kind of contraceptives prescribed (the Walworth clinic provided the larger Dutch cap, not the cervical cap that Stopes had designed herself). In 1921 Marie Stopes resigned from the Malthusian League and set up the Society for Constructive Birth Control and Racial Progress. By now she had also fallen out with Margaret Sanger, her American counterpart, who had inspired Stopes' work in earlier years.

Those who opposed birth control were organising themselves more effectively. The Roman Catholic Church had already condemned any use of contraception, and by 1921 had strengthened its campaign against it. An article by a priest appeared in the *Catholic Times* describing Stopes' birth control literature as '... almost incredibly obscene by its advocacy of unsocial and unnatural sin', anti-birth control letters were constantly appearing in newspapers, and the Catholic Truth Society published its own pamphlets opposing birth control. The Church of England was still opposed to contraception but its members were beginning to break ranks. The most famous of these was Lord Dawson, who was George V's physician. He told a Church Congress in 1921 that birth control was here to stay, and that 'no denunciations will abolish it'. The speech, by such a well-known and respected establishment figure, had a dramatic effect on public opinion.

More publicity for the cause came in a series of court cases during the 1920s, the most famous of which was Marie Stopes' case for libel against Dr Halliday Sutherland and his book *Birth Control: a Statement of Christian Doctrine against the Neo-Malthusians*. In the end she lost her case when it went to the House of Lords. The result was of great comfort to the Catholic Church, but the case and its outcome stimulated a great deal of public support for Marie Stopes and her campaign.

Birth control in women's control — feminism in the 1920s

The fight for birth control was taken up in the labour movement during a prosecution for obscenity in 1923 of two Communist Party members, Rose Witcop and Guy Aldred, for selling *Family Limitation* by Margaret Sanger. Witcop and Aldred had the support of the Labour movement newspaper, the *Daily Herald*, of many feminists and members of the Labour Party. Not surprisingly there was no support from Marie Stopes, given the politics of the defendants and Stopes' attitude towards Sanger. Her lack of solidarity with other birth control campaigners had been made obvious the year before, when she decided not to support a health visitor, Nurse Daniels, who had been dismissed for giving women information about where they could get contraception.

These cases motivated many socialist feminists to campaign for state provision of contraceptive advice. They rejected the eugenic approach, and instead saw control over reproduction as an essential aspect of women's autonomy over their lives. Men in the working-class movement were justifiably suspicious of birth control, since it was the working class who would be the target of any selective breeding programme if the eugenicists had their way. But there could be no equality for women unless they had the right to choose when and whether to have children, and gained freedom from a destiny defined by their biology, argued socialist feminists like Stella Browne, just as did the feminists of the 1960s and '70s.

By 1924, when the first Labour Government was elected, the campaign had been taken up by the Women's Co-operative Guild and many sections of the Labour Party and socialist movement. The Minister of Health was given a petition calling for welfare centres to be permitted to give birth control information. Though this was refused, pressure continued. In 1924 the Workers' Birth Control Group was set up, saying that 'all women, rich or poor, have an equal right' to knowledge about contraception. That same year the Labour Party women's conference voted in favour of contraceptive advice provided by local authorities.

Two years later, at the 1926 Labour Party conference, campaigner Dora Russell managed to secure victory over the National Executive Committee position that birth control was not a party issue. She called instead for the lifting of the government ban on local authority birth-control provision. Despite accusations of 'Neo-Malthusianism' the NEC recommendation had to be dropped – a great victory for socialist feminism.

Clinics for the poor

The voluntary sector was by now organising itself and creating a network of birth control clinics. The committee that had taken over the Malthusian League's Walworth Clinic set up the Society for the Provision of Birth Control Clinics (SPBCC) in order to establish birth control clinics for 'married women in poor circumstances'.

During the next couple of years a number of clinics were opened outside London. Many saw them as a way of putting pressure on central government. The campaign was gaining strength in the labour movement, but there was still no sign of the Ministry of Health shifting its position.

Opposition to contraception came from the Church and some members of the medical establishment, and there was a fear that provision of contraceptive advice would alienate voters. But in 1926 came the first sign of government change in position on contraception, when the House of Lords voted in favour of a resolution (from the vice-president of the Malthusian League) asking the government to allow welfare clinics to provide contraceptive information to married women.

But this did not prompt the government to change its policy. The voluntary sector was still growing, and the struggle continued to put birth control on the Labour Party agenda. The Labour Party resisted involving itself in what it saw as a non-party issue. This was despite the publication of figures showing that the rate of maternal mortality was rising every year.

By the end of the 1920s the campaign for birth control was vociferous, with considerable influence and increasing public support. After the second Labour Government was elected in 1929, a conference on 'Birth Control by Public Health Authorities' was organised by all the birth control groups and held in Central Hall, Westminster. This called once again for state provision of birth control for married women. Within months the Ministry of Health decided that local authorities could give birth control advice to women whose health would be put at risk by another pregnancy.

Following the issue of the Ministry of Health memorandum to local councils, the battle for birth control provision was fought in individual towns and cities. The voluntary sector was now organised by the National Birth Control Association (NBCA) which brought both campaigning groups and clinics under its umbrella. The association was committed to local authority provision, but would open its own clinics in areas where the district authorities did not do so. Starting in 1931 the NBCA set up a provincial network to press for local provision, in the form of both NBCA birth control clinics

and provision at Welfare centres, which would 'enable tl.
woman to obtain the advice now available to women rich end
pay a specialist's fee', as the Association said at the time. Oppo.
mainly came from the Catholic Church, which managed to stop
setting up of clinics in some areas, but by 1935 there wei
forty-seven NBCA and sixty-six council clinics in the country. But
still only a minority of women used them. Most working-class
couples prevented pregnancy by using either the condom or
withdrawal, and no clinic visit was needed for either of these.

The involvement of doctors, if any, tended to be only by those
few who were prepared to fit and prescribe a cap. Medical
organisations like the British Medical Association and the Royal
Colleges were not particularly interested in birth control, and did
not see a specific medical role in its provision. Some of their
members were openly hostile to contraception, believing it to
encourage immorality. Medical schools did not provide any training
for doctors interested in birth control, so the NBCA set up a training
programme for both doctors and nurses.

The one major setback for the birth control movement was an
under-population scare which hit Britain in 1936. Now the fear was
that 'the British race' would gradually diminish, and be sapped of its
strength. Statistics showing the falling birth rate were seen in the
context of an imminent war with Germany, where numbers were
rising in response to exhortations from the Nazi government.

The ideology of the National Birth Control Association had to
change. The fear of twenty years before – of a population explosion
amongst the working class – was overtaken by a sense of
vulnerability that now permeated the country in the midst of a
de-population scare. Straightforward 'family limitation' had lost its
appeal, and the interest and commitment of the NBCA had to
broaden. The rates of maternal mortality (both as a result of
childbirth and illegal abortion) were high, and many NBCA
members wanted the emphasis to be on women's health generally,
not just on birth control. In 1939, months before the Second World
War began, the Association changed its name and its aims. It was
now the Family Planning Association (FPA), and would provide
advice on birth control for married women who wanted to limit or

space their families, as well as setting up Women's Health Centres.

No new clinics were opened during the war, and there was also a shortage of rubber, which put contraceptive manufacture in jeopardy. The population scare continued, and the FPA widened its aims still further to include the encouragement of 'the production of healthy children who are an asset to the nation' and extended its work on infertility at a time when few doctors were interested in the problem – it has taken the high technology and publicity of the 1970s and 80s to secure medical interest in the area of fertility.

2
FAMILY PLANNING
Free and Easy

No attempt was made after the war to include contraceptive provision in the new National Health Service. Even though the aim of the NBCA had been for state provision of birth control, the FPA did not campaign for this now they had the chance. This was partly because the FPA felt it did the job better than the state sector, and also because, as birth control historian Audrey Leathard has noted, in her book *The Fight for Family Planning*, the then president of the FPA was personally against the NHS.

Clearly the FPA would have encountered considerable problems if it had campaigned for birth control to be incorporated into the NHS – the medical profession was still not interested, and religious objectors would have made the going pretty tough. But in retrospect it does seem remarkable that the FPA never once entered into any discussion with the government on NHS policy so that 'at no point was family planning even mentioned' during the NHS's setting up (Audrey Leathard).

The FPA's post-war emphasis was on clinics and the administrative network needed to maintain them. The population scare subsided as research made it clear that there was no dramatic downturn, and as the 1950s 'baby boom' began. It turned out that many people had simply postponed having children, rather than decided not to have them at all. Now that men had returned from the war, and the future looked more secure, the birth rate went up and up. By 1950 the association was running 100 clinics staffed by volunteer members of FPA branches. Some local health authorities ran clinics too, gave grants to help the association run clinics, or allowed FPA branches to use authority property. This pattern of provision continued for the next decade, with FPA provision continually expanding. By 1960 it was running 276 clinics and was seen as respectable and responsible by all but its most entrenched enemies. The Department of Health had no direct involvement in the FPA's work, but relations between the two were good.

New methods of contraception – the pill generation

In the immediate post-war years, only a minority of women were using the barrier contraceptives and spermicides provided by the FPA; the condom and withdrawal remained the methods used by most couples. But a revolution was on its way that would dramatically alter the nature of contraceptive provision and transform the lives of women – the introduction of the pill.

Research scientists had been trying to develop hormonal drugs to suppress ovulation since the 1930s. Researchers in Japan had found a way of extracting the hormonal compound diosgenin from the yam, and oestrogen had been extracted from pigs by American scientists. The original idea was to develop an ovulation suppressor drug which would be used as a treatment for gynaecological problems like painful periods. By 1951 Dr Carl Djerassi and other researchers working for the Syntex pharmaceutical company had discovered a way of making synthetic progesterone (which was called noresthisterone). It became clear that this drug was more than a gynaecological problem-solver – it could act as a contraceptive drug too.

American Gregory Pincus, working for the Searle Company, was also working on the development of hormonal contraception. Now with the support of Margaret Sanger, who secured financial backing from the foundation of a wealthy friend, Pincus and his colleagues M.C. Chang and John Rock worked on the development of a hormonal preparation that could be taken by mouth. Their first research paper on progestogen was published in 1956, and they went on to test the drug on women living in Puerto Rico and Haiti. During this research, it was found that the women had considerable bleeding problems, so oestrogen was added to regularise bleeding.

In 1960 Searle put Enovid 10, containing high doses of the progestogen norethynodrel and the oestrogen mestranol, on the market. The world's first generally available oral contraceptive was promoted after research on its effects on only 132 women, but with approval from the US Food and Drug Administration nonetheless. This new drug was first given to British women as Conovid in 1961, once the Medical Advisory Council of the FPA had decided it could be given to women at FPA clinics. Little was known about the effects of the pill, other than on ovulation. No large-scale research had been done, apart from the studies on effectiveness and acceptability done on Third World women and low-income women in Britain. (Some researchers began to find an association between pill-taking and cardiovascular disease, but no real conclusions on this were drawn until 1967.)

The steroid rush of the 1960s was on. Pharmaceutical companies in America, Germany and Britain were falling over themselves to make the most of what was clearly a lucrative market. By 1964 around 460,000 British women were on one or other of these early high-dose pills, and the numbers using barriers had dropped dramatically. The pill became the subject for hundreds of media investigations. Everyone wanted to investigate this new drug which was supposed to enable women to have sex without worrying about pregnancy, and therefore would make them sexually available to men at all times. The appeal was irresistible.

In common with US authorities, the FPA had decided that the pill could only be prescribed by doctors. Now contraception, which had been thought of by doctors as non-medical and irrelevant, was put in their hands exclusively. This medicalisation of birth control was as much of a social revolution as the supposed change in sexual behaviour that went with the pill. The medical profession retained their lack of interest in any other method – it was the pill they prescribed, and nothing else. The diaphragm was still provided by the FPA, but soon most of the women who used contraceptives at all were on the pill.

Doctors could prescribe the pill under the NHS if they did so on medical grounds. Otherwise it had to be on private prescription. This was probably why so many women at that time were put on the pill in order to 'regularise periods'. This rationale has led to much confusion, since the pill stops the natural menstrual cycle altogether, replacing periods with withdrawal bleeds. These bleeds are the body's response to a controlled dose of hormone, and are *not* periods, regular or otherwise. Neither does the pill have any long-term therapeutic effect on the menstrual cycle after it is stopped. But the myth persists.

By the end of the 1960s millions of women worldwide were taking the pill. But the link between high doses of oestrogen and cardiovascular disease had become clear, and in 1969 the first major 'pill scare' broke. Doctors were now being advised that they should prescribe lower dose pills (with 50 mcg of oestrogen or less), and manufacturers were working to discover what was the lowest dose possible which could maintain a contraceptive effect. This reduction in oestrogen level was followed in the late 1970s by sequential combination pills with a lower progestogen content. And other versions of hormonal contraception became available, which used a new kind of progestogen only and so did not carry the cardiovascular risks: the progestogen-only pill or mini-pill and the injectable contraceptive Depo Provera.

The 1960s also saw the introduction of the IUD into widespread use. After decades of research using devices made of various metals (see page 152), the first plastic device, in the form of an S-shape with a nylon thread attached, was designed by Dr Jack Lippes. The IUD, which needed no conscious involvement from the user apart from initial agreement to have it fitted, was thought ideal 'for use in under-privileged and less motivated communities', as birth control historian Elizabeth Draper puts it. The Population Council of America, which had sponsored research on IUD development, organised an international conference in 1964 to discuss research findings on the reliability and safety of the new device. The IUD was seen as a good way of reducing the size of the population in the Third World, where midwives and nurses could be trained to fit it as well as doctors, though in Britain it was fitted by doctors only.

At first it was thought that IUDs could only be used by women who had given birth, because it was difficult to fit them in those who hadn't. Smaller copper devices were introduced in the 1970s which could be fitted in women who hadn't had children, and became popular among young British women who didn't want to take the pill. But by this time it had become clear that the IUD carried an increased risk of pelvic inflammatory disease, and that one design in particular, the Dalkon Shield, was associated with terrible infection which killed many women. Only in the last few years has the story of the development and research of the Dalkon Shield been made public, mainly because of the cases against the US manufacturers A.H. Robins, brought by women who have suffered as a result of using it. More legal cases now are pending from women who have used other designs of IUDs.

The swinging sixties

Contraception was presented as safe and simple in the 1960s – if you were married. The FPA had modified its policy on suitable clients a little by saying that women who were about to be married could get contraception, but this was loosely interpreted by both contraceptive providers and women themselves. Boyfriends became 'fiancés' and mythical marriage plans were described by women who wanted the pill. Some FPA members tried to change the policy in 1964, but succeeded only in getting the association to back (in principle only) the setting up of Youth Advisory Centres. By this time Helen Brook, who worked at the Marie Stopes clinic, had decided to start special sessions for unmarried women. The sessions were held secretly to start with, but soon the story broke in the national press. Helen Brook left the Stopes clinic to found the Brook Advisory Centres, which started in 1964 and saw unmarried women who were under twenty-five.

The climate of opinion on sex before marriage was changing. The 1967 NHS (Family Planning) Act had made it possible for health authorities to provide contraception on NHS prescription, and for the unmarried. That same year the FPA decided to delete the mention of married women from its aims. In 1970 clinics were told that they could provide contraception for any woman, married or not.

There was another major change in the law in the late '60s – the

1967 Abortion Act. Until then legal abortion could be done only to save a woman's life, but women still sought and obtained illegal abortion. The safety of the operation was dependent on how much you could pay. Those who could afford nothing but a backstreet abortion risked infection, subsequent sterility, and even death. No one knew how many illegal abortions were performed every year, but it was clear that thousands of women had for years resorted to illegal abortionists and had attempted self-induced abortion. The high incidence of illegal abortion and its consequences was evident in research on maternal mortality and in the casualty departments of hospitals around the country.

The Abortion Law Reform Association (ALRA) had been formed in 1936 by socialist feminists Stella Browne, Dora Russell and others. At that time it was estimated that there were about 90,000 illegal abortions every year. Those who could afford it were able to have relatively safe operations, but others were forced to risk their health and their lives at the hands of the backstreet abortionist, or by trying to abort the pregnancy themselves. Abortion was raised in a series of legal cases and government investigations, and did much to strengthen the case for contraception to stop unwanted pregnancies. But no change was made to the abortion law itself. By the 1960s increasing numbers of doctors were prepared to perform the operation both privately and on the NHS. It became clear that the law was being broken on a massive scale, and by the mid-1960s ALRA was campaigning hard in Parliament, and getting increasing public support. The parliamentary arguments in favour of legal abortion had little to do with a woman's right to choose to control her own fertility, but instead involved a kind of pragmatic liberalism based on worry about maternal mortality, and the growth of the criminal abortion network. Parliament gave doctors, not women, the right to decide whether an abortion should be performed.

Population – free birth control and the numbers game

Over-population and the need for government steps to control population growth had, in the 1960s, again become a major issue, and provided a basis for the campaign for free NHS contraceptive services that started in the 1970s. The birth rate had been rising in Britain since the 1950s, and over-population, rather than the greed and exploitation of First World governments and capitalist companies, was presented as the major cause of economic problems in the Third World. The International Planned Parenthood Federation based in London, and the United States Agency for International Development (USAID), were running birth control projects throughout the Third World as if poverty could be relieved by simply reducing the numbers of the poor. (This attitude is still offensively apparent in a series of posters produced by the organisation Population Concern in 1986, aimed at raising money in Britain for population control programmes in the Third World. Using the slogan 'at this rate, one day there'll be more room inside than out' one poster shows the large pregnant belly of a black woman. At the top of the picture is a glimpse of her naked breasts, and, in the tradition of white racist representations of the yet-to-be civilised 'native', she is wearing a kind of loincloth made of string and calico. Superimposed on the lower curve of her belly is a graph showing the rise in world population between the year 1500 and the year 2000. 'Whatever your favourite cause – it's a lost cause', runs the text, 'unless we cope with the population big bang'.)

Free and comprehensive contraceptive services provided by the NHS, the campaigners argued, were the only way to achieve the 'zero population growth' needed in Britain with its limited space and resources. If unwanted pregnancies could be prevented, the population problem would be solved. In 1971 the Conservative Government was investigating whether Britain should have a population policy which would incorporate a birth control programme. The birth control lobby based its case on three main issues: NHS contraception and abortion services would, they argued, result in a cut in the abortion rate; provide immediate cost benefits for the nation by reducing the number of births and subsequent expenditure on the children concerned, and help to solve the population problem. Feminist arguments for the right to choose and the need for women to control their own fertility and sexuality motivated many of the campaigners, but were not used by the parliamentary lobby, which felt that such beliefs might alienate those in power and make it more difficult to win the case for comprehensive NHS birth control.

In 1972 Health Minister Keith Joseph announced that NHS contraception services were to be expanded, and soon afterwards the House of Lords voted for an amendment which would make contraceptives free on the NHS as part of the NHS Reorganisation Bill. The battle over free contraception continued in 1973 as the NHS Bill progressed in Parliament. A Labour Government had now been elected, and it was ready to respond to the increasing pressure for free birth control. Despite opposition from MPs like Jill Knight (an active anti-abortionist) and John Stokes (a right-wing moralist) as well as Catholic and other religious and moral objectors, the Lords' amendment was finally accepted, and contraception was henceforth to be provided free by the National Health Service.

Free contraception on the NHS meant a complete re-organisation of family planning clinics, many of which up till then had been run by the FPA. The FPA and the Department of Health worked out a process whereby responsibility for the clinics would gradually be handed over to the NHS. A scheme also had to be set up to enable the payment of GPs for providing a contraceptive service. In the end, after a long wrangle between the department of health and doctors, it was agreed on a scale of payments – Item of Service fees – depending on which type of contraceptive was provided. (In 1986 this stands at £8.55 per year for prescribing the pill or cap, and £28.70 for fitting an IUD.) GPs refused to prescribe condoms, and today condoms remain free only from family planning clinics. Many of the GPs had no training in providing contraception, and were not in fact able to fit caps or IUDs, so could only provide the pill. A 1976 survey by the FPA found that while around 90 per cent of the 23,000 GPs had registered to provide contraception, only a few thousand of these had been trained to do so. This explains the bias towards the pill still shown by many doctors – no special training is needed to write a prescription.

By the end of 1976 the FPA had transferred all its clinics to the NHS. Its new role was to be in education and information about family planning and, apart from running a few specialised clinics, not in direct provision of contraception. The FPA Education Unit was set up to provide courses for professionals (nurses, doctors, teachers and social workers) likely to be involved in sex education, and the Family Planning Information Service (FPIS) was set up by the FPA and the Health Education Council. The FPIS continues to produce information leaflets on contraceptive methods available at NHS clinics around the country, as well as a telephone information service for both contraceptive users and providers. The FPA, with the involvement of medical and other experts on contraception and contraceptive technology, still acts as an authoritative voice on contraception (both technology and provision) and initiates contraception and health education campaigns like the 'Men Too' project aimed to increase men's sense of responsibility for contraception (see page 36). It projects itself as anti-extremist and part of the establishment, a guardian of common sense on sex and contraception.

3

ACTION AND REACTION
Sexual Politics,
Feminism and the Moral Right

Even though the provision of free contraceptive services for all is now soundly established, it remains an area in which political battles continue. Feminists have raised issues of women's control and power over sexuality and reproduction which extend beyond the need simply to obtain the opportunity to avoid pregnancy. And the birth control establishment has now to contend with organised opposition from right-wing moralists who would like to see a return to 'Victorian values' and the family structure in which women have no choice but the role of subservient mother.

The women's liberation movement

Feminists had been involved in campaigns for birth control throughout this century and, with the rise of the Women's Liberation Movement in the late 1960s and early '70s, took on the issue once more. The focus of the struggle for control over our bodies was now the medical profession, pharmaceutical companies and the state, all of whom were seen as representatives of male power over sexuality and reproduction. For the first time in their lives, thousands of women were asserting their right to control their own fertility. Feminists were doing their own research into contraceptive methods and provision, and setting up information networks with an emphasis on self-help, not passive consumption of patriarchal prescriptions. Like Stella Browne in the 1920s, feminists saw their relationship to reproduction to be as political as men's relationship to production in the workplace. The personal was political, and women's struggle against male oppression involved a sexual as well as an economic revolution.

The most powerful expression of the new sexual politics came in the fight against proposed restrictions to the 1967 Abortion Act in the mid-1970s. Instead of looking to a small parliamentary lobby to safeguard the Act, women organised their own resistance movement – a broad-based mass campaign, open to all women. The National Abortion Campaign (NAC) was formed, made up of groups of women throughout the country who organised locally as well as nationally for 'free abortion on demand – a woman's right to choose'. The first national demonstration against James White's Abortion Bill saw thousands of women, many of whom had never before been politically active, marching for the sake of 'our bodies, our lives, our right to decide'. Feminists saw the struggle for abortion rights as having implications for the lives of all women, not just those who might choose to have an abortion. It involved an assertion of the right to sexual self-determination too, and this awareness was shown by the many lesbian feminists who were involved in the campaign.

The campaign against restrictive abortion laws was fought on many fronts. The Abortion Law Reform Association with its 'A Woman's Right to Choose' campaign organised parliamentary lobbies, and the Co-Ordinating Committee in Defence of the 1967 Act enabled many professional organisations which were concerned with birth control provision to put their case. Groups like the Labour Abortion Rights Campaign and Tories for Free Choice campaigned in the political parties. Socialist feminists (many of whom were in NAC) put pressure on all labour movement organisations to support abortion rights, and succeeded, in 1979, in getting the Trades Union Congress to sponsor a mass demonstration against the John Corrie Abortion Bill.

It became clear that the struggle for control over fertility involved more than the fight for abortion on demand. Feminists began to organise around the wider issue of *reproductive rights*, which was to involve work on injectable contraception, sterilisation, infertility and reproductive technology. Through the Women's Reproductive Rights Information Centre and other groups women were now able to discuss their own mixed feelings about fertility, and the political implications of age, race, class and physical disability in discussions and campaigns on sex and reproduction. With the growing awareness of racism, feminists began to question and attack population and contraception policies of governments both here and in the Third World, and moved beyond the individualism of 'a woman's right to choose'.

Modern opposition to abortion and contraception

The Roman Catholic Church had consistently opposed contraception with the view that sex was created for the purpose of reproduction, and that no mechanical means should be used to prevent conception. There had been organised opposition to the provision of birth control in the 1930s, and Pope Pius XI explicitly condemned the use of contraception as sinful. By the 1950s the church had modified its position a little, saying that the use of a fertility awareness method was acceptable, as long as sexual abstinence was used as a way of avoiding conception at the time of ovulation. The Church would never approve of sex that didn't involve intercourse as an option on 'unsafe' days.

The introduction of the pill precipitated a crisis within the Catholic Church once it was realised that many Catholics were using it. The proportion of Catholics on the pill was only slightly smaller than the rest of the population, and the debate went on throughout the early '60s, with many Catholics wanting their church's position on contraception to be relaxed. Finally, in 1968, Pope Paul VI issued the encyclical *On the Regulation of Birth – Humanae Vitae*. This encyclical attacked the use of all contraception, abortion and sterilisation, saying that artificial birth control was against God's law. The Catholic Church was split, with individual Catholics who wanted to be certain of avoiding pregnancy forced to flout their church's instructions.

The Vatican had more success in getting support for its position on abortion, which led to the setting up of organised campaigns around the world. In Britain the Society for the Protection for the Unborn Child (SPUC) was set up during the parliamentary debate on the 1967 Act, and went on to campaign for a restriction of the law as soon as it was passed. Repeated attempts were made to amend the Act throughout the 1970s, with three SPUC-supported MPs (James White, William Benyon and John Corrie) taking up Private Members' Bills in order to restrict the Act, and trying to stop women having access to abortion in all but the most extreme circumstances.

Another Catholic-backed organisation, LIFE, was also set up in response to the Abortion Act. As well as campaigning against the law, LIFE set up Lifeline, a counselling and support organisation which was supposed to help unwillingly pregnant women and deter them from thinking abortion was a solution. Lifeline provided hostels where women could stay until after they had had their babies. The organisation was aware that few women would seek help if they knew they would be told not to have an abortion, so it designed its advertising to look like that of the charitable pregnancy advisory services which could refer for abortion. If women really knew what Lifeline was, 'the phone would never ring', as LIFE's Nuala Scarisbrick said at the time.

Throughout the 1970s SPUC and LIFE organised demonstrations and the parliamentary lobby against abortion. In support of their case they alleged that the Abortion Act was being abused at virtually every level. In 1974 the *News of the World* ran a story by two journalists who claimed that the private abortion sector, in pursuit of financial gain, would diagnose a woman as pregnant and offer an abortion when she was not pregnant at all. The journalists, Michael Litchfield and Susan Kentish, went on to write *Babies for Burning*, a book which claimed that aborted foetuses were being made into soap, or thrown alive into incinerators, or being experimented on while still alive. Though it was later discredited, the book was a publicity coup for the anti-abortion organisations, who used it as the basis for their parliamentary and media campaigns.

Further allegations, mostly about late abortions, followed when attempts to restrict the law failed. These mostly involved stories of 'babies on draining boards' – live foetuses left to die in hospital sluice rooms after being aborted. None of these stories was found to be true. Having failed to make any substantial changes to the Abortion Act, the anti-abortion groups now campaign against reproductive technology and embryo research.

The moral right

The Catholic Church was no longer able to secure support in its hostility towards contraception from other Christian denominations. Protestants did practise birth control, with no instructions to the contrary from their churches. But a small wing of the Church of England did take up the fight against what it saw as the dangers of the sexual permissiveness that started in the 1960s along with the introduction of the pill. These groups saw permissiveness as a threat to the family, which was at the core of Christian society. The family was a sacred unit governed by absolute Christian values. Absolute values, by definition, cannot be questioned, and their rejection by anyone else was therefore intolerable. Increased availability of contraception and the new law on abortion weren't the only dangers, these groups believed – a series of legal and social changes on questions like homosexuality, divorce, mixed hospital wards, sex outside marriage, depictions of sex and violence on TV, and pornography, posed an equivalent threat to decent family life. The sort of liberal relativism and tolerance which says 'you stick to your beliefs and I'll stick to mine' had no place in a world ruled by God's absolute law – it was an insult and a sin.

The National Viewers and Listeners Association, headed by Mary Whitehouse, was the first of these groups to gain national publicity. Mrs Whitehouse had long been involved in moral campaigning, having been a member of the US-based right-wing organisation Moral Re-Armament (MRA) whose main commitment was to fight communism and its ungodly manifestations. While Whitehouse concentrated on 'cleaning up' television, other groups emerged. The Order of Christian Unity, founded in 1970, pledged itself to uphold God's commandments 'particularly in family life – education – and medical ethics'. The National Festival of Light was launched in 1971 with a London demonstration in support of 'Love, Purity and

Family Life', in opposition to those 'who are responsible for this moral breakdown of our society'. A network of Community Standards Associations was also set up, most of them based in towns in the Home Counties. Other small groups of moral campaigners (Bristol Family Life Association, Harrow Child and Family Protection League and For a Better Bromley) were also formed.

The Responsible Society, founded in 1971, decided from the outset to fight against 'the exploitation of sex' and for 'the encouragement of responsible behaviour in sexual relationships'. Whilst it had connections with other moral groups (at its first annual general meeting founder Valerie Riches talked about working in cooperation with groups like SPUC), the Responsible Society was the first organisation to concentrate almost exclusively on the issue of contraception and sex education for young people. The RS appeared to see itself as a cut above the other moral groups, with its bulletin subtitled 'for Research and Education in Matters affecting the Family and Youth', and proclaiming that 'approximately one third of its members' were 'doctors, teachers and social workers'. A series of academic-sounding papers were published: 'Sex, the child and the family; the role of the teacher', 'Children in society — state of emergency' and 'Sex Education, its uses and abuses'.

The Society's own view of what sex education should be comes across powerfully in 'But Where is Love?', written by Venetia Riches, daughter of RS founder Valerie. In the booklet are false claims 'that the overall failure rate (of the pill) is as high as 20%' and that babies born to women who had previously had an abortion were more likely to be premature and to suffer congenital malformations. The booklet is designed for use as part of sex education classes, and a list of topics for discussion includes questions like 'how would you feel if you were a bastard?' and 'when would groping in a writhing heap in the back of an Austin 1100 on Putney Heath have anything to do with love?'

Now the RS has moved into video production, with two programmes for use in schools. One, *Let's Talk about Love*, is a moral tale featuring a good girl who doesn't have sex and a bad girl who does. The good girl finally wins the sacred prize of a white wedding. (By this time she has already behaved in an arguably immoral and un-Christian way by refusing to offer any help or support to the bad girlfriend who is unhappily pregnant.) *The Great Population Hoax* is a more sophisticated attack on contraception and the family planning movement. It adopts anti-populationist arguments as a way of illustrating what the RS sees as a worldwide conspiracy to subvert absolute values. Valerie Riches has already made clear what she believes to be the nature of this conspiracy: she has drawn up a chart in which she links thirty-six organisations – including the FPA, the Communist Party and the Ministry of Overseas Development – which, she claims, promote sex education in pursuit of 'communism, humanism' and 'world domination'. It is this conspiracy which fires the RS – *The Great Population Hoax* makes no suggestion that the same First World capitalism which initiates population programmes is responsible for any other economic exploitation which needs resisting, or that women should have the right to control their own fertility.

Victoria Gillick and the under-sixteens

By the mid-1970s the target was what the RS called 'the family planning industry' and 'sex missionaries' – specifically the Family Planning Association and the Brook Advisory Centres. Whilst sex education remained a major preoccupation, the society had now decided to focus on the issue of contraception for under-sixteen-year-old girls. The subject of the attack was a Department of Health Memorandum to doctors which allowed the prescription of contraception without parental knowledge or consent to girls who needed protection from the possible 'harmful effects of intercourse', which meant pregnancy.

This was seen by the moral right as yet more direct state interference in the family. It was an ideological position which got broad support from the newly-elected Thatcher Government, which was also committed to reducing state involvement in health, education and social security, preferring to replace these state services with private companies and family support 'in the community'.

At the same time, Victoria Gillick started a campaign which she called 'Parents in Suffolk' which also wanted the 1974 Memorandum to be withdrawn. She started with an attempt to stop her local health authority from providing contraception for under-sixteens. A Roman Catholic, Mrs Gillick had previously been involved in LIFE, and in earlier years had been a member of Powellight, an organisation campaigning for repatriation of immigrants. Mrs Gillick now saw contraception for young people as part of a wider conspiracy which involved pharmaceutical companies, government and voluntary organisations in the aim of destroying the family unit by subverting parental control.

Mrs Gillick did what she could to get the FPA to incriminate itself, and to express what she believed to be its real and subversive motives. In 1979 she wrote to the FPA under a false name asking if she could be of 'assistance in any way', and requesting to know 'who are the members and friends of the FPA in Suffolk'. She also tried, through the Charity Commissioners, to remove the FPA's charitable status. These attempts failed.

Victoria Gillick and her ten-strong family (which she originally thought to be a media liability and had tried to conceal from the press) soon began to get national coverage. The campaign against contraception for under-sixteens was already popular with both the national and local press, who seized any chance available to publish stories about 'Teeney' or 'Gymslip' sex, in which contraceptives were called 'sex aids' and which were often illustrated with pictures of depressed-looking teenage girls in short skirts. With the arrival of Mrs Gillick the press could use 'Why mother is right', and 'Parents hit back' headlines that gave the 'teeney-sex' story an extra punch.

After her failure at local level, Mrs Gillick's next step was to attempt to deal directly, in the courts with the DHSS Memorandum (amended in 1980 to say contraception should only be given without parental consent in 'exceptional circumstances'), and to get legal backing for her demand that none of her daughters would be given contraception by her local health authority without her consent. She had support from the Responsible Society, who produced a pamphlet *No Entry for Parents*, in which Mrs Gillick's 'independent and heroic stand' was praised, and a series of allegations were made about what was called the 'Child Sex Lobby' (made up of all those who were in favour of contraceptive advice for young people). The RS and other moral right organisations had embellished the anti-family world-domination conspiracy theory with what they believed was a secret campaign by paedophiles to have legal and government-supported access to young children. This had begun by removing parental control and providing contraception, and young people's demand had been created by sex education, or 'value-free instruction on deviant behaviour', as *Times* columnist Ronald Butt describes it.

Mrs Gillick was the first moral right activist to take on the state. What followed is well known – at first she lost her High Court case, but won it on appeal. The Department of Health took the case to the House of Lords, which finally ruled against her.

Holding on to the middle ground

Mrs. Gillick may have seen her defeat as a triumph for permissiveness, but much of the language used by her opponents differed little from her own. The message was clear – sex for under-sixteen-year-old girls is dangerous and undesirable, but teenagers are going to do it anyway so they ought to be protected from its worst excesses. The rights of doctors to exercise 'clinical judgement' were also seen to be at risk. 'Anti-pill group threatens GPs' was a typical headline from the medical press.

Although they wanted to retain the power to decide whether teenagers should be given contraception, the liberal establishment was united in its belief that sex before the age of sixteen was an unquestionably bad thing. The British Medical Association said 'early sexual intercourse is undesirable, both medically and emotionally' but supported the DHSS Memorandum by pointing out 'there is no evidence to suggest that lack of contraception deters girls under sixteen from having sex. Moreover, doctors, parents and social workers would still be left "to cope" with these casualties.' It was also once again assumed that those who need protection by professionals are economically deprived and lower-class – they are 'disadvantaged young teenagers' (Brook), or they 'come from disadvantaged backgrounds' (FPA). Many individuals within the establishment opposition to Gillick may have had other more progressive views, but felt forced to express only those opinions that tied in with the prevailing ideological climate if there was to be any hope of hanging on to the DHSS Memorandum.

Throughout the under-sixteens debate girls were presented as victims who were, as the FPA put it, being 'pressured by the media, advertising, the pop industry and their peers into having sex before they are ready'. But no definition was provided of what being 'ready' for heterosexual intercourse actually meant, or who might be qualified to say whether any individual was 'ready' or not. Perhaps more important was the lack of evidence for the much-discussed psychological and emotional damage that could be expected in an under-sixteen-year-old girl who has sex with her boyfriend, and which could be proved to be exclusively and especially experienced by girls in that age group, and not by women who are one, two, ten or thirty years older.

After the Gillick campaign the FPA moved further to the right in the debate that followed on sex education and the 1986 Education Bill. In a letter to Education Secretary Kenneth Baker FPA General Secretary Alastair Service distanced himself from 'extremists on both sides'. In what one assumes to be a reference to the book *Jenny lives with Eric and Martin* (about a girl who lives with her gay father and his lover), Service refers cryptically to 'publications' which cause 'understandable anger among many reasonable people', and claims that such material is 'inappropriate and can cause offence'.

Worst of all was the lack of discussion of the double standard on which so much of the under-sixteens debate was based. The Gillick campaign focused on girls, not boys, and the liberal opposition followed suit. No one suggested that under-sixteen-year-old *boys* ran risks (physical, emotional or psychological) if they had sex, and that they might or might not need protection – this was, as the BMA president said at the time, a 'side issue'. Young girls might be seen as sexual innocents, at risk of being defiled, but boys were perceived as somehow *already* sexual, with nothing to lose.

Young girls were not encouraged to see themselves as having the right to choose or to feel responsible about sex, because the idea that they may actively want and enjoy a sexual relationship was intolerable for their elders. But it's difficult to see how anyone can feel confident and sure about saying 'no' until they have the power to say 'yes'. Now, after the defeat of the moral right lobby, it is clear there is a need for much more discussion and debate on young women's and men's sexuality that goes beyond the terms set by Gillick, the Responsible Society and the liberal establishment's defensive campaign. They are all fighting over the middle ground of an ideological and political territory in which young women will always be passive and vulnerable victims, and which does not include questions of genuine choice, responsibility or self-determination.

The campaign against sex education has now been overtaken by the need to educate young people about AIDS. This cannot be done effectively without explicit descriptions of how the HIV virus is transmitted, and what 'safer sex' involves. It is clear that the taking of individual responsibility by all sexually active people is the only way of limiting the spread of AIDS, rendering the moral right campaigns for parental power and control over what their children are allowed to know an irrelevancy.

The gains for women secured by this century's campaign for birth control have been considerable and, despite the moral backlash, most have been maintained. We do have the opportunity to control our own fertility, even though ultimate power over it still lies in the hands of doctors and of the state. Whether you have access to safe, early abortion still depends on what part of the country you live in, and on your doctor's attitudes. Fewer than fifty per cent of all abortions are done by the NHS. And even though we can use contraceptives that are almost a hundred per cent reliable in preventing pregnancy we have no control over the multi-national companies who decide what kind of contraceptives will be researched and how and for whom they will be marketed.

The arguments that have won over the church, state and medical profession to support birth control have had nothing to do with women's rights or our sexual liberation, but have been eugenic, populationist and essentially economic. No one would suggest that the Conservative Government maintains free contraception on the NHS for the sake of sexual, reproductive or any other kind of freedom for women. The government has, after all, made a series of moves which are essentially anti-woman in its policies on the welfare state, and in its pressure to get women out of the workplace and back into the home. It blames the 'decline in moral standards' and the 'permissive society' for the failure of its own policy on law and order, and the rise of crime, violence and riot.

But the economic benefits of providing free contraception are clear – it costs far less than the abortion, maternity, housing, education and other services that may be needed otherwise. The eugenic arguments in favour of limiting births among working-class and young people may also play a part. When Conservative Keith Joseph said, in 1974, that 'our human stock is threatened' because a 'rising proportion of children are being born to mothers least fitted to bring children into the world', his backing for birth control was in complete harmony with those early eugenicists who feared they would be overrun by the lower classes.

Women have yet to achieve the right to true reproductive self-determination, even though, as individuals, we may be able to use the facilities available in a way which gives us limited control.

4

THE POLITICS OF INFORMATION

'Any idiot can get a girl into trouble, don't let it be you'

(FPA slogan to encourage male responsibility for contraception)

In 1985, for the first time in the history of the birth control movement, men became the target of a propaganda campaign. The contrast with what over the years had been produced for women was remarkable. Not only were men being motivated to take positive responsibility, but to develop qualities which they 'are often encouraged to suppress: warmth, tenderness, sensitivity and openness in their relationships'; (FPA document on the philosophy and aims of the 'Men Too' campaign).

But girls still got 'into trouble'. They were still victims, who were dependent on protection from the men they had sex with (or at least the man who wasn't an 'idiot'). Women have yet to be given the opportunity to take genuine control over reproduction, and instead we must look to men, be they doctors, politicians or boyfriends, to provide us with the means of defence against what is seen as a wayward and ruinous fertility. No one has ever addressed our finer feelings unless they might affect our compliance with a birth control regimen and result in our risking pregnancy.

Motivation – who needs it?

An enormous amount of energy has been spent on motivating women to use contraception. Although no one could doubt our individual motivation (just think what lengths we went to and the physical risks we took in order to avoid having children before the medical and political establishment got involved) somehow it has been thought necessary to persuade us to have fewer babies. The focus of these campaigns has always been specific groups of women who are deemed both unfit to reproduce and not intelligent enough to take the initiative in avoiding pregnancy. Middle- and upper-class white women were able to get contraceptives and pay for safe abortion without needing motivation from the birth control movement (see page 5), but working-class (and now black and young) women were seen as requiring someone else to get them to do so. So as part of a policy of *population management* rather than simple control of numbers, the birth control propaganda machine focuses on the less fortunate whose fertility must be controlled, and who don't have the wit or means to take control themselves.

So while early feminist campaigners concentrated on practical provision of contraception for the women who actively *wanted* it, those whose groups evolved into the present-day 'family planning' organisations worked hard on persuading women who, they had decided, passively *needed* it. Information and propaganda had to be produced for these women, not in the cause of enabling them to take power over their own fertility, but to keep them in order.

Once the medical profession got involved, this control extended to all women, regardless of class, race or position. Women didn't need to understand the mechanics of contraception, all they had to do was cooperate and comply. Gradually contraceptive methods were developed which needed less active and day-to-day involvement by the women who were using them, with increasing control being taken by the providers. This is even promoted as an advantage for women by those who distribute the IUD and hormonal contraception. Now it is the same group of women (the lower racial class – however that is defined), who were originally the target of contraceptive propaganda, who are now most likely to be given contraceptives over which they have the least active control and which will be effective whether or not they are given information about it. So doctors are advised that for 'mothers of large families, of children in care or with very little care, those with haphazard personal and social relationships, in trouble with the law, and with substandard living conditions ... methods such as the IUD or the injectable which do not require the patient's cooperation are often best' (section on 'poorly motivated patients', *Handbook of Family Planning*, 1985).

The changing influences on contraception information

Although population management is still the ethos behind all birth control agencies (it is the point of all the information they produce, and the reason why they get state funding), the last ten years have seen a considerable change in their attitude towards women. Starting in the late 1960s, feminists began to learn more and raise questions about fertility control, and rejected the right of doctors and governments to make decisions, for women. Feminists were not satisfied with bland reassurances about the effects on health of contraceptive methods and, on the basis of lived experience, did not accept cheerful exhortations like 'Enjoy life with family planning – contraception is simple, safe and it works!' (FPA 1977). The birth control agencies had no choice but to respond (in part at least) to these new demanding consumers, who would not be satisfied by simply being told to go back to their prescribing doctors when contraception didn't deliver its supposed life-enhancing qualities. Women were learning too much, and would not necessarily cooperate with instructions like this one on the IUD: 'If the unpleasant effects go on for long or if the IUD comes out the *doctor* will advise whether a different one should be tried or whether you should use some other kind of contraceptive' (FPA 1976 – my italics).

Those who produce information material on contraception for the FPA and other organisations have become increasingly aware that women want more, not less, to read about each contraceptive method before they make a choice. This awareness has come largely as a result of the influence of feminism, and the way in which the women's movement has set up its own information network on birth control and women's health generally. Feminists who are not doctors, social workers or population planners have been motivated to do their own research and produce information about contraception with the aim of giving women more knowledge and thus more individual control over their fertility. The title of a book like the collectively written feminist health manual *Our Bodies Ourselves* clearly shows this commitment, and it is one which has been to some extent taken up by other information providers. And although some doctors and health educators still believe that women should not be told too much, and that the reader of the new FPA leaflets will be discouraged from using contraception by being informed about some of its disadvantages and negative effects on health, consumer testing done whilst the leaflets are in preparation shows the opposite.

But pressure comes also from the moral minority, which wants to restrict anything that it sees as providing the potential for giving women control over their sexuality and reproduction. They fear that a right to choose means women will reject traditional roles, and the white Anglo-Saxon Protestant (WASP) family structure – what the Responsible Society calls 'the fabric of ordered and responsible relationships which has been the basis of our society' – will be subverted and ultimately destroyed, so that women will no longer want the role of motherhood 'acknowledged to be the most wonderful and rewarding in the world'. The moral right is essentially concerned with suppressing information about sex and contraception, because it appears to believe that information about contraception creates a demand for sex that would not otherwise exist. This must be to some extent a strategic decision, but it also shows their belief that the area of information is the most powerful element in the subversion of moral values. So instead of launching a campaign, for instance, to stop free contraception in this country, it tries to stop sex education and to restrict the right of young people to be told about contraception without their parents knowing. It does not try to fight the pharmaceutical companies that produce the pill, but instead expends an enormous amount of energy campaigning against one single sex education book for young people, *Make it Happy* by Jane Cousins, as if the information within it has the power to destroy all civilisation.

But the moral right's influence does manifest itself in the way that centrally coordinated control is exerted over much of the information we get. The Advertising Standards Authority and the Independent Broadcasting Authority impose codes of practice and standards over what goes out in the media, so that, for instance, the TV Public Service Announcement on male responsibility and contraception could only be screened after 9 p.m. Extensive advertising of cigarettes and alcohol is allowed at sporting events, but the BBC refused to screen a race in which a car with 'Durex' written all over it was competing. Many advertisements for contraceptive services and abortion referral agencies are forced to be coyly ambiguous for fear of offending what the controlling authorities deem to be good taste. Both the Department of Education and Science and the Department of Health have the last word on what information should be given to young people in schools, with the result that sex education should now be given 'in such a manner as to encourage ... pupils to have due regard to moral considerations and the value of family life' (1986 Education Act). Organisations like the FPA and Health Education Council are dependent on government funding, and so have to conform to departmental requirements. So it was that the FPA was requested to withdraw *Make it Happy* from its booklist.

The fear of the information bodies is that because the moral right, although tiny and without mass support, has the ear of government it poses a genuine threat to the existence of organisations like the Brook Advisory Services, the FPA, and to contraceptive provision in general. What cannot be achieved directly by the moral right is effected by self-censorship – during the Gillick campaign, the FPA withdrew an information leaflet for teenagers before anyone had requested it to do so. All the establishment groups opposed to Gillick took on the language of the moral right as a defence against her. So the Department of Health backs confidentiality for young women because without it they might not seek professional advice and 'could then be exposed to the immediate risks of pregnancy and of sexually transmitted disease as well as other long-term physical, psychological and emotional consequences which are equally a threat to stable family life'. And while the FPA used to extol the benefits of sex within a 'loving and caring relationship for young people, two new virtues have since been added. What is promoted now is sex that is part of a 'loving, caring, *responsible and lasting*' liaison (my italics).

Sex, politics and the status quo

The Department of Health, the medical establishment, the FPA, Brook and others have little to fear from the moral minority. They do none of the things the moral right accuses them of doing, and have never attempted to bring about the sexual revolution the moral right so fears. The cause of young people's right to confidential information and practical advice on contraception is far less important to them than the doctor's right to take action to prevent pregnancy in young women. And once again, it is always the teenagers from 'disadvantaged backgrounds' who are presented as being most in need of this protection. And though the desire to prevent accidental pregnancy is overriding, there has never been any suggestion in information material that these groups might encourage the kind of relationships and sexual practice which would remove or reduce the likelihood of conception – lesbianism and homosexuality, or even heterosexual sex without intercourse.

The status quo of heterosexual society is continually reinforced by the information we get, and the view of women's sexuality it communicates. The fact that a contraceptive 'does not interfere with intercourse' and allows sexual 'spontaneity' (see page 48) is presented as an unquestionable 'advantage'. It is assumed that our priority is to be protected against conception in such a way as to ensure that we can be swept off our feet according to the rules of romantic love. There is no attempt to free women from passivity and sexual oppression and to present alternative advantages – like being in control of both fertility and what kind of sex we have, and when. This maintains the patriarchal view that women are sexual victims, and reinforces the fear of sexual autonomy that we often have. It's as if the nature of female sexuality cannot be redefined, and what counts above all else is that we don't get pregnant as a result of expressing it.

The need of family planning organisations and doctors to prevent pregnancy is so powerful that it manifests itself almost as an irrational fear. The impression given is that accidental pregnancy is the worst thing that could ever happen to a woman, and that abortion is an absolute disaster. Family planners find it intolerable to think of women consciously deciding to terminate a pregnancy, even though what may be the repeated early abortions that occur when we use an IUD or some contraceptive pills are quite acceptable to them. This is not because these abortions are early and so physically safer, it is because we don't know about them. Early abortions that we *do* know about, in the form of menstrual extraction done before a pregnancy is confirmed, are illegal.

So none of the information bodies even tells us about abortion until we are unwillingly pregnant, because it has been decided that abortion should not be explicitly acknowledged as a form of birth control. Information leaflets about barrier methods do not say that a diaphragm or cap with abortion as a back-up (to its around three per cent failure rate) is the physically safest reversible way of avoiding pregnancy, presumably because too many women might then consider abortion as an option *before* they were already pregnant.

Does it work – is it safe?

This selective way of dealing with information also results in confusion between what's *safe* and what's *effective* as a contraceptive method. This confusion is rarely addressed by contraceptive providers and informers. All too often we are led to believe that the avoidance of conception – the effectiveness of a method – is the overwhelming priority, without being given a real opportunity to assess its safety. Because abortion is not supposed to be an actively pre-meditated decision, we are encouraged to use the contraceptive methods likely to pose the greatest risk of everything else *but* pregnancy and abortion.

Once we are using these methods – we are on the pill, injectables, implants or IUDs – a new priority takes over. The information we get has to be steered along a narrow course which will give us a good deal of the facts we require about the methods, but controlled in such a way that we don't get frightened off them.

But doctors and family planning agencies have little power over what emerge as 'scare stories' about contraception in the press, television and radio. When the discovery of a link between the pill and breast and cervical cancer hit the front pages in late 1983, they were entirely unprepared. Family planning doctors and GPs were in the front line as many of their patients sought informed reassurance or clear details of the health implications of the new findings, which many doctors had neither read nor understood. The FPA urged women to stay on the pill until the research findings were investigated because otherwise 'the risk of pregnancy could be very high'.

Despite the FPA's attempts to allay fears, the popular press, with its traditional love of contraception stories with their mixture of sex, health scares and the likelihood of reader identification, continued to run stories that were guaranteed to disturb. 'Pill revolt by wives' (the *Mirror*) and 'Scandal of birth pill wives in cancer alert' (*Sunday People*) were typical, notable too because of the way in which those who took the pill had taken on the status of 'wife' now that they might be running health risks, when usually such papers prefer to give the impression that the pill is taken only by 'gymslip pill-girls' who want unrestricted sex. 'Today the three and a half million women in Britain who are on the pill are confused and frightened … and with good reason' led the *Daily Mail*'s feature on the new research, a statement bound to be at least as influential as any doctor's words of comfort to a thirty-year-old woman who'd been on the pill since she was a teenager.

The FPA responded to the scare a few weeks later with a leaflet called 'Pills in Perspective'. The phrase 'in perspective' is one which is often used by the information-givers when they are writing about scary or unpleasant aspects of a contraceptive. It seems to be a way of telling us that it is unreasonable and rather silly to be worried in the first place. The leaflet briefly outlined the 'two much disputed unconfirmed reports' and, though it was acknowledged that 'any woman who is very seriously worried about *any* method of contraception would be advised to seek an alternative making sure there is no gap in contraceptive protection if pregnancy is undesired', we were also told (with no evidence for such an assumption) that 'in fact, most women will continue pill use and watch for any new reports'. Later we were informed that the pill protects against some other forms of cancer, as if this was some compensation for running the suspected risks of cancer of the breast or cervix.

Information breakdown

Much of the rest of the information we get is often confusing and inadequate. We are frequently given the pill by doctors who have had no general training in contraception, and who have no idea how to prescribe and fit other methods and don't know much about them. The more knowledgeable doctors and information-givers sometimes choose to withhold certain information because they have decided it is not in our interests to know it, or that we can't be trusted if we are told the full story. Consultant gynaecologist John Guillebaud stresses in the introduction to his book *The Pill* that 'We live our lives and base our decisions on what we know, and the best and right decisions are those for which we feel we have taken responsibility', but even he does a remarkable about-face when telling us about morning-after contraception: 'You will notice that I do not name the pill brand(s) used,' he says, adding, 'This is deliberate. Readers should resist the temptation to "dabble" in this kind of treatment, without medical supervision'.

Others do more to confuse than to inform. Dr David Delvin in his 'no-nonsense guide to taking Britain's most popular and effective contraceptive', *Taking the Pill*, answers the question 'will the pill make you sexier?' by the one-word answer 'yes'. A footnote supports his assertion by saying that 'studies do appear to show that women who are on the pill do have intercourse considerably more often than women who haven't got such good contraceptive protection', though 'in fairness' he 'must admit that a very tiny number of women feel *less* sexy on the pill'. What can we conclude from this? Is it that frequency of intercourse equals being 'sexier' or that being protected from conception makes some women less sexy? And can this really be called *information* at all? It is of no use to any woman who is experiencing the loss of libido which has been confirmed to be linked with pill-taking.

Still more confusing and unhelpful is the advice in yet another 'no-nonsense guide' to birth control by Dr Michael Smith, honorary chief medical officer of the FPA. In *Woman's Own – Birth Control* a mythical patient complains, 'I have tried five different sorts of pills but they all give me side effects. My boyfriend won't use french letters and I can't face the thought of a cap or an IUD. What shall we do?' Dr Smith cannot bear such negative thinking on contraception, and shifts the blame back on to his patient. 'Whilst many people think to themselves that they would rather not have to use contraceptives because all have disadvantages, they accept what is best for them pretty quickly and do not keep presenting it as a problem.' He goes on: 'It is understandable that you do, though, because unconsciously you may be blaming your contraceptive method for your deep distress over sex generally. It is just possible, for instance, to find that somebody who wants to reject every method of contraception as unsuitable is unconsciously rejecting *heterosexual* relationships.' Smith saves himself from outright heterosexism by bouncing the responsibility off the patient and on to the 'attitude that society has taken for so long towards homosexual relationships'. It turns out that this is why 'it is more acceptable to blame the contraceptives than to accept that your heterosexual relationship is not right for you'.

It is not only the pill that is the subject of misinformation. We may still be told (as we were by the FPA in the 1970s) that 'if you do become pregnant with an IUD in place it won't harm you or your baby in any way'. Translated this means that if you don't have the device removed and your pregnancy is not one of the 50 per cent with IUDs in place which will miscarry, or the 5 per cent which are likely to be ectopic, then you and the baby will be okay. And it's worth remembering that even though the FPA regularly updates its contraceptive method leaflets, many doctors and clinics continue to distribute out-of-date information material, waiting until stock has been depleted before getting new editions, no doubt in the cause of 'efficiency savings' – even though they pay only postage costs on the material they get. (You can check the date of publication on FPA material by looking at the back of the leaflet – for example one produced in January 1987 will be marked 1/87.)

The messages that accompany the facts we get on contraception are largely dependent on the beliefs and bias of the information giver. The FPA in its leaflet on injectable contraception, such as Depo Provera (DP), points out that when a baby ingests the small amount of hormone passed through breast milk 'this is thought to be harmless to the baby', whereas the Women's Reproductive Rights Information Centre says 'it is not known whether this has any effect on breastfed babies'. This remark is part of a section on when 'it is not advisable to use DP'. The two statements are factually similar, with both telling us that there is no evidence for any harm being caused, but the context, implications and conclusions are very different – one reassuring, one not. Sometimes the message is even more subtle. The FPA's 'Right methods of birth control' leaflet in its section on Depo Provera states: 'Opinion differs about its value.' This could equally well be said (but isn't) about every other method listed, but comes across as a coded message that warns the reader about Depo Provera in particular but without saying why.

Given the nature of information about contraception, with its complex mixture of medical facts, political attitudes and beliefs, and issues of individual power and control, what can we do to ensure we make positive use of it? Clearly different information networks have different aims, and different criteria of what constitutes 'informed consent'. Information can never be value-free, and the status and aims of the person or organisation giving it will always affect our perceptions of what we learn. Our choices may not always be based on an apparently rational or objective assessment of information – the fact that a friend had a dreadful time with an IUD may have much more influence on us than any amount of statistics which show that such an experience is unlikely to happen to us.

We have to take individual initiatives and learn to weigh up and exercise our own priorities. We can make use of a wide range of resources – the Women's Reproductive Rights Information Centre, Women's Health Information Centre, Family Planning Information Service, our GPs and family planning doctors, books about contraception and women's health, and friends. In the battle for women's control of our own fertility, knowledge is power.

5

CHOICES
Sexuality, Relationships, Reproduction

The point of using contraception is to be able to have sexual intercourse without getting pregnant. It's a technical means to an end, developed and controlled by doctors, pharmaceutical companies and governments. But women's needs and interests are very different from those of these three groups. We don't use contraception in order to reduce world population, or because we want to save the government money. Neither do we use it because we want to add to the profits of multinational companies or support this new area of medical control. We use contraception because we want the pleasure and intimacy of sexual intercourse with a man, without becoming pregnant.

Contraception and sexuality

Those who provide contraception hardly ever mention sex in an explicit way, even though it's fundamental to the use of contraception. What they are interested in is our fertility and its control, not our sexuality. It's as if they think sex is something that happens instinctively and without conscious thought, desire or choice. And we have to be prepared before being overtaken by the uncontrollable carnal rush which obliterates the intellect.

Pregnancy can only happen as a result of one sexual act – intercourse. The unspoken message from all the agencies involved in contraceptive provision is that intercourse is all we ever do, and that

47

this is the immutable core activity of heterosexuality. As Germaine Greer has pointed out, our sexual priority is assumed to be *intromission* – the ejaculation of semen into the vagina. This assumption is continually reinforced by contraceptive propaganda. 'Men who care' according to the FPA, 'use the sheath', as if men have no choice or control over where they ejaculate. A man who cares might be equally well advised to come anywhere but in his partner's vagina, but no one dares subvert what seems the natural order of sexual activity.

The rules we learn about sex and contraception are clear. Sex begins with 'foreplay', which can include a range of activities which get us ready 'to go all the way' with intercourse and intromission. From the moment foreplay begins we lose the power of conscious and deliberate thought, which is why it's best that we contracept well in advance of the tidal wave. The best contraceptive is therefore the one that is least evident at this time, the one that 'does not interfere with making love'. We can be trusted not to become pregnant as long as the decision to use contraception is made well away from sex, so are advised to put in a diaphragm hours before the act occurs, take our pills as part of a nightly routine, or be protected from pregnancy every hour of every day with an IUD. We are promised that as long as we do this, sex can be 'spontaneous' (the word that covers all things sexual in family planning literature) and our minds can be the necessary blank.

This consistent denial of our ability to make decisions about what we do and when we do it is a crucial part of attitudes to romantic love and the role that women have within it, and is tremendously difficult to fight. Many of us fear we'll be thought calculatedly lustful if we have contraceptives with us the first time we sleep with a man. We prefer to seem 'carried away' by the supposedly unpredictable mood of the moment (unpredictable even though it is meant to involve the same sexual act every time) and to be untouched by the sordid practicalities of contraception. Within a long-term relationship we may want to hide ourselves in the bathroom when we put in a barrier, so as to emerge unsullied and ready for true romance.

We are encouraged to feel that the ideal contraceptive is one we either don't have to think about at all (like an injectable contraceptive, implant or IUD), or one we only think about outside the context of romance and sexuality (the pill). And, since no contraceptive provider seems to believe we would want to take conscious responsibility for contraception, we get no opportunity to discuss how it can be integrated into our sexuality, and what the benefits may be of a sexual practice that includes more than sexual intercourse. Sexuality is taboo even when it directly affects the experience of using a method, such as the taste of spermicides. Few contraceptive-prescribing doctors would be prepared to talk about oral sex, let alone advise us to delay the putting in of a barrier until we're going to have intercourse – they're worried that we'll lose all sense of responsibility once sex begins and will forget about contraception altogether and so get pregnant.

Contraception and reproduction

The idea of 'virility' involves a bringing together of the sense of male fertility and male sexuality. There's no word or notion that provides women with an equivalent sense. Men don't even have to father a child to have this sexual/fertile awareness. Whilst many of its manifestations – machismo, male aggression and violence – are negative and oppressive to women, at best it can represent an integration of reproductive and sexual confidence and potential.

Women have learned that their fertility is a liability which makes them vulnerable, not powerful. Many of us feel that menstruation is a source of shame, cyclical rhythms a sign of unreliability. Using contraception can distance us still further from our own reproductive potential, even lead us to denying that it matters at all. Many who use contraception have no idea of whether or not they are fertile, and those of us who use what are the most effective methods in preventing pregnancy (the pill and other hormonal methods) lose all opportunity to experience any evidence of our menstrual and potentially reproductive cycles. We have no way of knowing whether we are fertile or not.

The desire to know that you are fertile can have nothing whatsoever to do with wanting to get pregnant and have a child. It is an understandable and legitimate desire, not necessarily irresponsible. The idea of making a child with the man you love can be very exciting, even though neither of you has any intention of doing so for several years, if at all. We can be pleased and excited to be pregnant and to have confirmation of our fertility and still choose to have an abortion. But many of us who have these feelings are unable to admit to them for fear that we'll be deemed irresponsible and confused. It's especially difficult to explore these complex emotions when so often we are treated as careless or deliberately troublesome when we don't use contraception, or thought to be lying when we say we've used contraception but the method has failed.

Current contraceptive methods can provide us with the freedom not to reproduce when we don't want to, but the loss of a knowledge of our fertility can be part of the price we have to pay. We may feel cheated when we've used contraception for many years thinking that we can get pregnant as soon as we make the choice to have a child, and then find we have to wait many months or years before we get pregnant. Our fertility may even be decreased by the method we use, or it may turn out that we have been infertile all along. Propaganda for contraception often gives the false impression that we can have as much control over getting pregnant as we do over avoiding pregnancy.

Men and contraception

Most women feel that contraception and reproduction are ultimately their responsibililty, and with the advent of methods like the pill and the IUD this has been accentuated. It has always been women who get pregnant, have an abortion, or give birth and look after children. Now, with modern methods of contraception, it is usually women who take responsibility for birth control too. Although in principle we may want men to share the responsibility for contraception, and be relieved when we find a man who will make that positive commitment, we know that in practice it is our bodies and our lives which are most at stake. He can *choose* whether to be involved – we have no alternative.

How much you can share the decision about contraception depends on the kind of relationship you have with your sexual partner, as well as what practical contribution he is prepared to make. Will he use a condom, or have a vasectomy if sterilisation is an option? Is he willing to learn about fertility awareness methods, to keep track of your menstrual cycle, and be happy to abstain from sexual intercourse during the fertile days? How much does he know about the pill and the IUD – and how much is he prepared to learn? Can he tell whether you've put your cap in correctly? Has he talked about what he'd want and how he'd feel if you got pregnant?

If you are not in a steady relationship or this is a new involvement, it may be more difficult to share the responsibility. In the past many men assumed that if a woman was going to have sex then she must have got contraception 'sorted out' and so didn't even ask about it. The advent of AIDs has changed this to some extent. You are now much more likely to have a discussion with your partner about safer sex as a way of avoiding the transmission of the AIDS virus. This may lead you both to talk about contraception too.

Women have fought, and are still fighting, for the right to control their own fertility. It will take many years (and a revolution in contraceptive technology) before the majority of men will share genuine responsibility for birth control. Men have to challenge and change traditional attitudes towards both their own and women's sexuality too. It is up to them to take this initiative – women can't do it for them.

Deciding issues

A decision about contraception involves thinking about your health, sexuality, relationships and morality, which will all act as influences on which contraceptive you choose, and how you choose it. And the way you juggle these elements, and the conclusions you reach, may vary throughout your reproductive lifetime, and reflect other changes in your life.

Few women are able to choose between all the available methods of contraception. You may be too old to take the pill, or maybe you are planning to become pregnant at some time so can't consider sterilisation. You may have had gynaecological problems which mean you can't have an IUD, or be in a relationship with a man who won't use a condom. 'Choice' may come down to having to make a decision between two methods, neither of which you really want to use at all.

Some of our needs may seem contradictory. For instance, it is clear that the physically safest form of birth control is using a barrier method, with early abortion as a back-up if the barrier fails. But even the small risk of accidental pregnancy (around 3 per cent) may be intolerable for you if abortion is not an alternative, either because of emotional or moral reasons or because you know it would be difficult to get the operation where you live. You could find that the reliability of a contraceptive method may, in the end, be your major priority and, despite your worries about possible health risks, it may become clear that the pill is your best option. Or your concern for your health may still override any other factor, and you decide that the small risk of pregnancy with a barrier is one worth taking.

It may help to see the choice you are making now in the context of your whole reproductive lifetime – which may be three decades or more. Whilst you don't need to make decisions now about what contraceptive you might use in twenty years' time, it is worth thinking about whether and when you'd like to have a child, and how long you would want to stay on any particular method. Of course your plans could change completely, and for all sorts of reasons, but it still could be useful to have some idea of your needs both now and in the future.

Seeing the doctor

If you are thinking about using the pill, IUD or a barrier you will have to discuss this with the doctor who will prescribe it for you – either your GP or one at a family planning clinic. Whilst FP doctors should be well-informed about contraception, and what kind of screening and follow-up care you need, many GPs are not. The majority of GPs have not had special training in contraceptive provision, and some may behave as if your need for contraception is some kind of illness for which prescription of the pill is a cure.

It's worth talking to friends about which local doctor they see for contraception, and what the doctor's attitude is like. How much information does the doctor provide, and is he or she open to discussion and questioning? Does the doctor do the regular check-ups you'll need, and what kind of response can you expect if you have problems with a method? You can also find out for yourself (by asking at the clinic or surgery) whether your GP has had any training in providing methods apart from the pill. This is especially important if you are thinking about having an IUD – ideally the doctor should have had both training and continual practice in fitting the device (see page 157).

A supportive doctor who can provide the help you need to come to your own decision, and feel happy with it in the long term, is invaluable. At the very least you should be able to feel confident that you are getting adequate information and proper care, and that you'll be treated with respect and taken seriously if you have any problems with the method. The doctor should also be prepared to do the necessary regular check-ups you'll need, especially if you are going to use the pill or IUD.

Contraception and disability

Not everyone with a physical disability will need to take this into account when deciding on a contraceptive method. There may be no reason why your choice, and the factors you consider when you make it, should be any different from those of able-bodied women. But some methods are unsuitable for women with particular disabilities or medical histories – check in the following sections on contraceptive methods to see if any of these apply to you. It really depends on the nature of your disability, as well as how much practical help and support you have from your partner.

It's especially important to find a sympathetic doctor who will do his or her best to offer the widest choice possible, and will accept your sexuality and need for contraception without question. Many health professionals still find this difficult, and assume that you are somehow asexual just because you have a disability. Others may be particularly keen for you to use the combined pill or be sterilised, acting as if they think you are 'unfit' and therefore should not have the opportunity to reproduce. A GP whom you trust, who knows you and your medical history may be the best person to see, but a good family planning doctor should be able to understand the relevant facts and help you in your decision too.

Contraception and AIDS

The disease AIDS (Acquired Immune Deficiency Syndrome) is likely to have a profound effect on all our sexual and health priorities in the coming years. So far its impact in Britain has been mainly on the gay male community, intravenous drug users and men with haemophilia. But the Human Immunodeficiency Virus (HIV) which may lead to AIDS can be transmitted between heterosexual partners just as it is between gay men, and can be contracted by anyone.

AIDS demands honesty between partners. Both need to know what health risks each might be taking in having sex together, and most importantly whether either has other sexual partners. We need to have 'safer sex' if there is any risk of transmitting the virus. Although it is thought that HIV is transmitted more easily through anal sex, it can be passed through vaginal intercourse and oral sex too. Sex will be safer if the man uses a condom. It is not clear at this time whether particular brands of condom are better than others in preventing the transmission of HIV. It also appears to be worth using a spermicide – those containing Nonoxynol 9 (see page 66) are known to kill the HIV virus in laboratory conditions in very weak concentrations, and probably do so when they are in the vagina too.

It may be that in years to come we will use barrier methods like the condom and spermicide as prophylactics (protectors against disease) as much as we use them for their contraceptive effect. A woman may choose to use the pill, IUD or sterilisation but still ask her partner to use a condom because of its prophylactic effect. We may develop different routines depending on the nature of our sexual relationship: if it is long-term and monogamous we may decide not to use barriers as well as other methods of contraception; if it is a casual short-term relationship we may want to use prophylactics. At the time of writing, condoms are free only from family planning clinics, but in the future GPs may be able to provide them for prophylactic as well as contraceptive purposes.

If we already have HIV we are more likely to develop full-blown AIDS if we get pregnant, so contraception is especially important. The virus has a fifty per cent chance of being passed to the baby, who could also develop AIDS and die very young. If it is known that you have the virus and you are pregnant you are likely to be pressured very strongly to have an abortion.

It is difficult to foresee at present (when the total number of people in this country who have contracted AIDS is only in hundreds) what steps all of us will need to take in relation to AIDS in the months and years to come.

Contraception and abortion in Ireland

Contraception in Ireland is legally available for 'bona fide' family planning purposes. This has been the law since 1979, but it has never been clearly defined. Religious objections to contraception mean that there is no government involvement in or funding of family planning services, and those that do exist are likely to be in larger towns and run by non-profit making-independent organisations. There is a total of fourteen clinics in Ireland at the time of writing.

A minority of Irish GPs and pharmacists will also provide contraceptives. You will have to pay – whether you go to a private family planning clinic or to your GP. Services *do* exist and are helpful and supportive, but access to them remains a problem – women who live in country areas may have no way of getting to a clinic and be unable to get help from a GP.

Sterilisation is not covered by the 1979 Family Planning Act, so in theory there should be no problem in obtaining it as a method of contraception. In practice however, hospital ethical committees will not permit sterilisation and it is done only at two private hospitals which have very long waiting lists. Irish women who want to be sterilised often come to England for the operation. Vasectomy is available at some of the private family planning clinics.

Irish women come to England for abortions too, since it is illegal in Ireland. It is impossible to know how many women make this journey every year, but an estimate of around 10,000 seems about right. In the past many were referred through Irish counselling services, but this was made impossible after a court ruling against any abortion referral. A special support group (based in London – see address list page 210) for Irish women coming to England for abortion now helps with referral to clinics and provides emotional support too. Many Irish women will continue to make their own way, sometimes with the help of friends who live in Britain once they arrive.

Contraception after childbirth and at the menopause

Each section on the different contraceptive methods that follow includes information about the difference that individual health needs might make to your choice. But to provide a short-cut if you have just had a baby or are experiencing the menopause, some of this information has been extracted to create this separate section. It may be useful to read it before you read the method sections.

When you've recently had a baby

It may be some weeks after giving birth before you want to have sexual intercourse, although fertility can return very quickly. But your body is still going through many changes, and your contraceptive choice has to take this into account.

Breastfeeding can suppress ovulation and so act as a contraceptive, but you cannot rely on this unless you are feeding on demand, and doing so at least every four hours, day and night. This frequency of feeding and nipple stimulation results in an increase in the level of prolactin which is thought to stop ovulation. Less frequent breastfeeding may delay ovulation and menstruation, but it cannot be relied upon to stop it altogether.

You cannot use the **combined pill** if you are breastfeeding because it is likely to reduce the amount of milk you produce. If you are bottle-feeding you can start the combined pill within a week of the birth.

The **progestogen-only pill** (POP) does not reduce lactation, but a small amount of progestogen is likely to be present in your breast milk and passed to the baby. There is no evidence at this stage that this poses any long-term harm to your child (see page 139). You can start taking the POP 48 hours after the birth. You should not use injectable contraceptives (Depo Provera, Noristerat) until six weeks after delivery. The bleeding problems that can happen with injectables are more likely at this time (see page 146).

You would also have to wait at least six weeks before having an **intra-uterine device** (IUD) fitted. The risk of perforation and expulsion is much greater if the IUD is inserted into the soft post-natal uterus and before the cervical opening has begun to close. An IUD should be fitted only when your uterus has returned to its normal size – if it's inserted before that time you should make sure the doctor is very skilled and experienced in IUD-fitting and that you have regular check-ups to see that the device is still in place.

It may also be difficult to fit a **diaphragm** at this time, especially if you have torn during delivery and the scar tissue is not fully healed. Even if you are able to have a fitting soon after delivery the shape of your vagina can change during the next few weeks and you may need more than one size of diaphragm over a short time.

Sterilisation immediately after childbirth is more likely to result in physical problems, especially bleeding and thrombosis. You are also more likely to regret the decision if there is no interval between birth and sterilisation, and this is the case with vasectomy too (see page 168). It is better to wait for a while before making this decision, and you should make this clear to any doctor who appears to be pressurising you into having a sterilisation straightaway.

Regardless of what method you want to use in the long-term, the **condom** together with spermicide is probably the best option if you want to use a barrier, or while you're waiting until you can go on the combined pill or be fitted with an IUD. You could also use **spermicidal foam** or **withdrawal**, but neither of these are as reliable as the condom.

Fertility awareness methods can also be used after childbirth, but only if you have already had experience of using them, and are skilled at recognising your own personal signs of fertility.

Contraception at the menopause

Once the menopause is over, and it is clear that your periods have stopped altogether and you have ceased ovulating, you no longer need contraception. This can happen at any time in your 40s or 50s, but may be preceded by several months of irregular or light periods. The menstrual cycle could become very long, or you could have frequent bleeds.

Since it is so hard to tell whether or not your last period was the final one you will still need contraception during this time. If you are in your 40s you should use contraception *for two years* after the last menstruation. If you are 50 or over you should use it *for one year* following the last period. If you still haven't had a period by the time this year or two has elapsed you needn't use contraception any more. But until then ...

Doctors now suggest that if you are a non-smoker you can use the **combined pill** until you are 45. The risk of thrombosis and other cardiovascular problems is increased as you get older, so you should switch to another method once you are over this age. Smokers over 35 run the same risk of cardiovascular disease, so should stop the pill at that point. It is impossible to tell whether or not the menopause has started if you are on the combined pill, because it suppresses the menopausal changes.

You could use the **progestogen-only** pill right up until the menopause, but once again you won't be able to tell when it's happening. The only way is to go off the POP every couple of years and see whether your periods return. The POP does not pose the same risks of thrombosis associated with the combined pill, and so can be a very good option for older women. It also appears to be more effective in preventing pregnancy in older women whose fertility is decreasing.

You can use an **IUD** until it is clear that your periods have stopped completely, and as long as you have no problems with the device. Uterine changes during the menopause can result in pain if you have an IUD, so return to your clinic or doctor if this happens to you.

Barrier methods (condom, cap or diaphragm) can also be used through the menopause. You could find you have some vaginal dryness, and so want to use a lubricant like KY Jelly as well as a spermicide. Changes in the vaginal surface can also mean you are more likely to be sensitive to the spermicidal chemicals, and experience vaginal irritation and soreness. A spermicide-free condom used with KY Jelly may be the best option if this happens to you. Vaginal dryness doesn't always happen – continued and frequent sex (either with your partner or with masturbation) helps to maintain vaginal lubrication through and beyond the menopause.

PART TWO

6

BARRIER METHODS

A contraceptive that is used only when it's needed, and is not active inside your body every moment of every day, makes basic sense. Barriers were the first contraceptives used; along with spermicides made of natural substances like lemon juice and vinegar, they gave generations of women a chance to control their fertility.

These were what we started with, and were what, at the end of the last century, were developed and manufactured by promoters of birth control. Use of barriers reached a British and American peak in the 1950s, but in the 1960s, with the introduction of the pill and the IUD, both the use of and research into these methods went into decline. It's really only the condom that has remained popular. It's still almost as frequently used as the pill in Britain.

Using a barrier requires conscious control – you have to make a decision to use it each time you have sex. Other contraceptives, like the IUD and the pill, protect you from pregnancy whether or not you are having sex, and the decision to use them is made away from the context of sexual desire and arousal. This is one reason why these methods have not been strongly promoted – prescribers worry that the method is too open to unreliable use. It's also the main reason why some women dislike the method: they feel the element of calculated decision- making undermines the spontaneity of sex.

It's been assumed that this pattern of use has recently changed, and that women have turned to barriers because they are worried about the possible health risks associated with other methods. But surveys of contraceptive use show that this is not the case – the diaphragm and cap are used by less than 2 per cent of women.

Young women in particular are even less likely to use these barriers than they were ten years ago. But even some of those doctors and drug companies who in the past promoted other methods will admit the future lies in the development of barrier methods. There is more research into new designs, and an up-dating and marketing of a centuries-old method, the sponge.

But barriers still tend to get treated as second best, okay if you can stand the mess and inconvenience, and only suitable for a certain kind of woman. It's been said that to use a barrier a woman needs 'a stable relationship and a bathroom' as if it will revolt all but the most devoted man, and that it's dirty.

Advice and information almost exclusively concentrate on the practical aspects of using a barrier, and not on what women feel about using the method or what effects it might have on our experience of sex. Many women have no doubt that barriers are reliable, but never get a chance to discuss what may be their major concerns – questions of aesthetics, how they might affect sexual practice and enjoyment – so never try them. Others, who do use barriers, have usually had to learn to incorporate them into sex without much help from information-givers or prescribers.

The standard suggestion is to put in a barrier well before sex begins, or even before you think it's likely. Every night, as part of a regular routine, you contracept. Or you can put in the barrier up to three hours in advance of the time you might have the supposedly 'spontaneous' sex. All of this is to be done in private, on the assumption that you will no longer be desirable if you're seen to be taking practical steps to prevent pregnancy.

There are a number of disadvantages to this approach. Far from being able to forget about your barrier once it's in place, you'll have to be aware of how many hours have elapsed since insertion, and put in extra spermicide if it's more than three. Perhaps more important, advance contraception rules out oral sex for many couples because the spermicide tastes so awful, so our ability to choose what kind of sex we want is undermined.

You don't need to put in a barrier except when you are going to have your partner's penis in very close contact with your vulva or inside your vagina, and he is going to have an orgasm. Intercourse may be only one aspect of sex for you, and you may not want to do it every time. When you do, you can use a barrier. This does mean thinking about contraception in the midst of sexual arousal, but if the cap and spermicide are easily available, and you are confident that you can put them in with ease, there need be little interruption of lovemaking. After all, the person who is using contraception is the same person as the one who is having sex – there is no need to separate the two realities.

Some women *do* dislike barriers because they find them intrusive and a turn-off. No amount of saying how putting in a barrier need be no more of an intrusion than taking off your clothes is going to make much difference if you hate using a barrier. But it is an attitude that has been learned, and is continually reinforced by many doctors – a part of the range of feelings of shame and embarrassment which a patriarchal society has constructed around women's sexuality. And it can change.

This is not to say that contraception could become in itself erotic, only that there is no need for it to be perceived as irrevocably anti-erotic. One way or another the method will have to be integrated into your sexuality if you are to feel good about using it. You may decide you are happier to separate the sex from the contraception and put in the barrier in advance. You may want to do this at some times and not at others, or alternate with your partner what kind of barrier you use, condom or cap. You could also combine barrier methods with fertility awareness, and use a barrier only in the middle of your cycle, when you are likely to get pregnant (see page 98). What's important is that you should make your own choice about how you deal with it, one that feels easiest and most relaxed for you.

Barriers as prophylactics

Over the next few years there is likely to be a considerable change in the use of barrier methods, especially condoms. Instead of being used for the purposes of contraception they will be used for prevention of the spread of the sexually transmitted virus: Human Immuno Deficiency Virus (HIV), the virus that can lead to Acquired Immuno Deficiency Syndrome (AIDS). The condom was initially used as a prophylactic, and it looks set to return to its original role.

New designs of condom are likely to become available. The spermicidal chemical Nonoxynol 9 (contained in many brands of spermicides, see page 66) is known to kill HIV in laboratory conditions, and is therefore likely to do so in humans too.

Whether an AIDS-prompted increase in the use of barrier results in a decrease in the use of other contraceptive methods remains to be seen. It may well be that we choose to continue to use other methods for contraceptive protection, but use condoms and spermicides as well when we need them as prophylactics against sexually-transmitted disease. Those of us in monogamous long-term sexual relationships may not change or add to our contraceptive methods.

The diaphragm

85–95 per cent effective

These barriers are made of rubber, and various designs and sizes are available. There's a bit of confusion between diaphragms and caps – often both are called caps although the designs are very different. The larger dome-shaped diaphragm has a reinforced rim which helps it stay in place over the cervix. The smaller cap fits more snugly over the cervix, so doesn't need the reinforced rim.

Getting a diaphragm fitted

Diaphragms have to be fitted by a trained doctor or nurse who'll know how to check which size you need. Too big and the device won't sit behind your pubic bone and will feel uncomfortable; too small and it won't act as a proper barrier over the cervix. A spermicide will be prescribed at the same time.

The size of diaphragm is measured by its diameter – they are available in sizes from 50mm to 100mm. The average size is 70-80mm. Nowadays it is almost impossible to get half sizes, and the gradations increase in 5mm stages: 70, 75, 80, for example. It used to be possible to obtain a 72.5, which for some women was ideal, but no more.

The choice of diaphragm and of spermicide can't really be specified in advance. There are three types of diaphragm rim: the flat spring, coil spring and arcing spring. Some women find the arcing spring easier to insert, some find the softer coil spring less likely to press on the urethra and so cause irritation or bruising leading to cystitis (see page 80). If neither of these considerations makes much difference to you to begin with, simply take what you are prescribed and see how you get on with it. But remember you can always try a different design if you have problems.

Types of diaphragm

Brand name	Design	Sizes available
All flex	arcing spring	65-95 mm
Durex	arcing spring	60-95 mm
Durex	flat spring	55-95mm
Ortho	coil spring	55-100mm

The front of the diaphragm should fit neatly behind the pubic bone, the back behind the cervix and against the vaginal wall. It should be the right size to retain its shape at the same time as not being too small and likely to shift off the cervix. You'll be shown how to put it in and remove it (see page 68) and how to check it's in place. You may be given a practice diaphragm to try at home – usually for a week – so you can leave it in overnight to confirm that it's comfortable.

Once you've been given a new diaphragm you may be asked to return to the clinic in a few months' time to check you're still happy with the method. Assuming you are, there is then no need to have a check-up more than once a year *unless*

- You have been pregnant and you've had an abortion, miscarriage or given birth
- You were fitted before you started having regular intercourse – the size and shape of your vagina can change when you have regular sex
- You have lost or gained more than 3kg (7lb) in weight

All of these could cause a slight change in your internal dimensions. Weight loss, for instance, can mean you need a larger diaphragm because the space inside your vagina could have got slightly bigger.

These changes can happen anyway, regardless of weight change or pregnancy, so the diaphragm size does need to be checked once a year. The diaphragm itself may need replacing too.

Spermicide is available in the form of cream or jelly, foam or small pessaries. Foams are the most reliable, especially for use without a barrier (see page 79). A spermicidal jelly provides more lubrication than a cream. There is now a spermicide on the market (Gynol II) which isn't artificially perfumed, but it still smells and tastes of the spermicide itself. The rest of the products have a cosmetic scent and taste.

Spermicides that can be used with diaphragms and caps

Brand name	Spermicide chemical	pH
CREAMS:		
Delfen*	Nonoxynol 9	4.5
Duracreme	Nonoxynol 11	6.0-7.0
Orthocreme*	Nonoxynol 9	6.0
JELLIES:		
Duragel	Nonoxynol 11	6.0-7.0
Gynol II*	Nonoxynol 9	4.5-4.7
Ortho-Gynol Jelly*	Nonoxynol 9	4.5
Staycept Jelly	Octotoxynol	4.25-4.7
FOAMS:		
Delfen Foam*	Nonoxynol 9	4.5-5.0
Emko foam	Benzethonium chloride	7.4-7.8
PESSARIES:		
Double Check*	Nonoxynol 9	4.25-5.25
Ortho-forms*	Nonoxynol 9	4.0-5.0
Staycept pessaries*	Nonoxynol 9	4.25-5.25

* *These contain Nonoxynol 9 which may kill the AIDS virus – see page 64.*

The pH of these spermicides varies slightly from product to product, with some more acid, some more alkali. A pH of 7.0 indicates a neutral state, where acid and alkali are equal. The higher the pH, the more alkaline the spermicide; the lower the pH, the more acid it is. Some women find particular spermicides can irritate the vagina and vulva. If this happens to you, try changing to a brand with a different pH. You can also be allergic to the spermicide itself, so you could switch to one containing a different kind of Nonoxynol than your current brand.

Using a diaphragm and spermicide

It is not known exactly how much spermicide is really needed, though you'll probably be told to apply 5-10cm to both sides of the diaphragm, and to smear some around the rim. This instruction is almost certainly over-cautious, and it may be that simply applying spermicide to the side of the dome that sits against the cervix will be enough, with perhaps the addition of a little around the side of the rim which is behind the cervix. Research is under way into whether any spermicide is needed at all, but since microscopic sperm seem likely to be able to swim between the rim of the diaphragm and the vaginal wall using none at all may well decrease reliability.

The spermicide is active for three hours, during which time you can have sex once. Intercourse after the three hours is up, or more than once in the three hours, means you should put in extra spermicide (see page 69). This too is cautious advice – research has shown that spermicide can be active for several hours longer. But the lack of conclusive evidence on this means that it's best to rely on the three-hour instruction until we definitely know different.

Once you have applied the spermicide, choose whichever position is most comfortable for you to insert the diaphragm. You may want to squat, or to stand with one leg up with your foot supported on a bed or chair, or it may – if you are already in bed, for instance – be easiest to lie on your back with your knees up. Find out by experiment which position is easiest. Then:

1 Separate the lips of your vagina with one hand. With the other press the sides of the diaphragm together between your thumb and forefinger.

2 Gently push the diaphragm into your vagina, and up and back to cover the cervix and to sit behind the pubic bone.

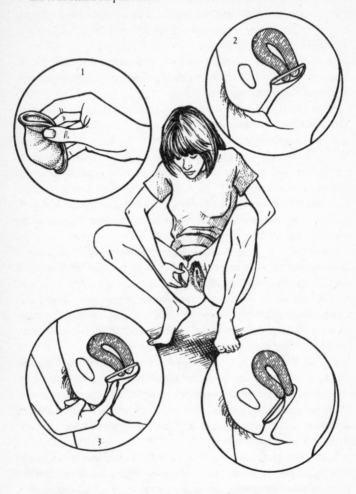

3 Put your finger inside your vagina to check the diaphragm is covering the cervix. You should feel a fleshy protrusion a bit like the end of your nose.
Wrong. The diaphragm is too far forward. The cervix isn't covered and the rim is in front of the pubic bone. It will probably feel uncomfortable too.

Some women find insertion difficult at first. Try a few times on your own and not when you are planning to have sex. It can be difficult to get a grip on the diaphragm when it's covered with slippery spermicide, especially if there is a lot on the rim. So if you do use spermicide on the rim, try to leave a bit of it uncovered so it's easier to hold and insert.

Insertion may be more difficult if you have any disability that affects co-ordination or dexterity, or if you have a visual disability. In this case your partner could help you put in the barrier. The doctor or family planning nurse should be able to show him how to do it, and how to check your cervix is covered. It's vital that you feel confident he knows what he's doing. There may be a risk of dislodging the diaphragm if you empty your bladder using the Credé method (manual pressure on your abdomen), so check it's still in place afterwards.

It doesn't matter which way round the diaphragm is inserted (dome facing the cervix or the other way round), as long as there is spermicide on the side next to the cervix.

It is sometimes suggested that you should not have a bath once you have put the diaphragm in. The spermicide could get washed away, or the diaphragm be dislodged. Bathing during the six hours after intercourse is also advised against for this reason. If you are already aware that water gets inside your vagina it is probably worth taking this advice. If it doesn't, it is okay to bathe. Showers are fine, however, as the water can't get inside your vagina.

You can now have intercourse once within the next three hours. If you do it more than once, or more than three hours after putting in the diaphragm, add more spermicide. Vaginal pessaries may be the easiest for you to use, or you could add more cream or jelly using an applicator which your doctor can prescribe when you get the spermicide.

The diaphragm must be left in place for a minimum of six hours after intercourse. It should not be left inside you for more than 24 hours without removing and cleaning it. If you have frequent intercourse during a single day this could be impossible, though you could try to time it so that you leave at least one six-hour gap, after which you can wash the diaphragm and re-insert it.

Remove the diaphragm by hooking one finger under the rim and gently pulling it out. It will still be covered with some of the spermicide, as well as some semen. Wash it in warm water with a small amount of unscented soap, and dry it gently before putting it back in its box. Never boil a diaphragm, or use disinfectants to clean it. This can damage the rubber. There is no need for the diaphragm to be sterile, but it should be clean. It's also worth checking for little holes or tears in the diaphragm dome after you've washed it. And if the outer side of the dome (immediately next to the rim) looks uneven or puckered you should get a replacement.

The Cap

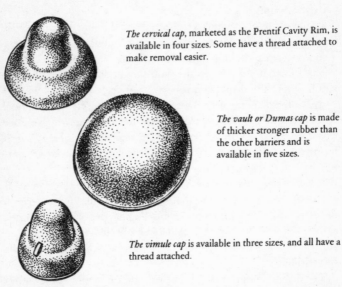

The cervical cap, marketed as the Prentif Cavity Rim, is available in four sizes. Some have a thread attached to make removal easier.

The vault or Dumas cap is made of thicker stronger rubber than the other barriers and is available in five sizes.

The vimule cap is available in three sizes, and all have a thread attached.

There are three kinds of cap: the cervical cap; the vault or Dumas cap and the vimule cap. (You can use any of the spermicides listed on page 66 with a cap.) All of them are held in place on the cervix by suction. They don't press on the vaginal wall, but do protrude further down into the vagina than does a diaphragm. These caps used to be widely available in this country, but are now often provided only if you cannot use a diaphragm. You may be offered one if your vaginal muscles aren't strong enough to hold a diaphragm in place, or if you have a prolapsed uterus or one that tilts backwards instead of forwards. All these conditions could make it difficult to fit a diaphragm.

The cap does have some clear advantages over the diaphragm, and should be as widely available. Less spermicide is needed, and the fact that it doesn't press on the vaginal wall makes it a good option if you are prone to cystitis (see page 80).

But some people do believe a cap is less reliable. Failure could occur if it is dislodged from the cervix during sex, and you may not realise this has happened. The cervix can change its shape and position during the menstrual cycle, and it has been suggested that women could have two sizes of cap for use at different times of the cycle – if you have a *very* sympathetic doctor it might be worth asking for two fittings.

Fitting a cap

Being fitted with a cap and being taught how to use it may take longer than getting set up with a diaphragm. The doctor or nurse will need to make sure it's the right kind and size of cap for your cervix. Insertion and removal (especially the latter) can be more difficult to learn. All of these are reasons why health professionals are often less keen on prescribing caps, and why you may have to persuade the doctor or nurse to fit you and teach you how to use it. It is therefore worth seeking out a doctor or nurse who regularly prescribes both the cap and diaphragm, who is likely to have both the necessary expertise and enthusiasm for the method.

Not all women can use caps. If you have a pelvic infection (inflammation of the fallopian tubes, ovaries or uterus) or cervical disorder or malformation you probably won't be able to, or at least you'll have to wait until the condition has cleared up.

How to use a cap

It has been suggested that caps can be used without spermicide, on the assumption that the cap creates an effective barrier in itself, and

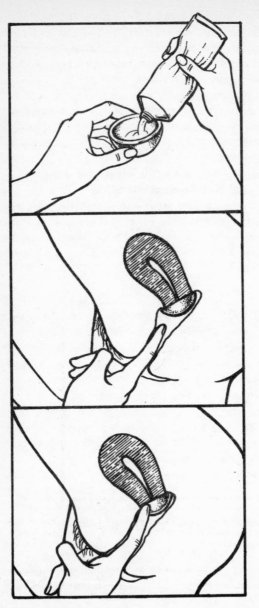

1 Fill the cap one third to one half full of spermicide, taking care not to get any on the rim. Otherwise it could slip off the cervix.

2 Insert the cap into the vagina and carefully guide it over and on to the cervix, where it will secure itself by suction once you take your fingers away.

3 Check it is in place by running your finger round the edge. Do this again if you have intercourse more than once while it's in.

sperm cannot travel past the rim. But until research confirms this it does seem advisable to use spermicide, and to add another lot of spermicide after three hours or if you have intercourse more than once during those three hours, in the same way as you would with a diaphragm.

The cap should be left in place for six hours after intercourse. As with the diaphragm, you should not leave it in longer than 24 hours. Women do say that the vagina begins to smell unpleasant if the cap is left in place for longer than a day, so it makes sense to remove it within 24 hours. The effects of the cap on the cervix if it is left in place for a long time are not known, but there is a possibility that continued suction could lead to cervical lesions.

Removing a cap can take some practice, as you have to break the seal created by the suction before you can get it out. If the cap has a string attached this might make it easier.

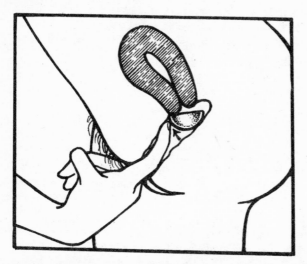

Insert your finger and tip the cap off the cervix, then remove it from the vagina. You can bear down as if you are having a bowel movement to make the cap and cervix lower in the vagina and easier to reach.

The honey cap

This is a kind of barrier that is available from only a few doctors in this country, and not on the NHS. A 60mm arcing spring diaphragm is used, which is soaked in honey before being inserted. The idea of the honey cap is that it can be worn more or less continuously for a year after it has been soaked in honey by the prescriber. There is little information on reliability, but one research trial was stopped because the pregnancy rate was so high. It is not known what effect the honey might have on the vagina.

The cap or diaphragm and sexual pleasure

You should not be able to feel either the diaphragm or cap when it's inside you. If you can feel it you may need a smaller one, or have put it in wrong. Some men say that they are definitely conscious of it during intercourse, or rather that there is greater sensation of the penis without a barrier than with it. The only way to discover whether this is a particular disadvantage for you is to try it. Some men say they can feel that the barrier is in place during intercourse. The sensation is usually described as one of awareness, rather than anything that mars sexual pleasure. If you decide it really does interfere with sex you may prefer to use another method. The sponge, for instance, is much smaller and you are both less likely to feel it. But then it is also less reliable ...

The sponge

The contraceptive sponge, called 'Today', is the most recent addition to the range of barrier methods. It does not need to be fitted by a doctor, but can be bought from family planning clinics or a chemist. It is not generally available free from clinics like other contraceptives.

The sponge is round and one-size, measuring about 50mm across by 20mm deep, and is impregnated with spermicide. It is made of polyurethane, and has a polyester loop attached to make removal easier. An indentation on one side enables it to sit on the cervix.

Once the sponge is in place you can have intercourse as often as you like for the next 24 hours. You have to leave it in place for six hours after intercourse. So if your last intercourse was exactly 24 hours after insertion you then wait another six hours before removal.

The sponge has then been inside you for a total of 30 hours, which is the maximum it should be left in place.

Trials in the US suggest the reliability of the sponge is about the same as other barrier methods, but the result of British trials is not so encouraging. The sponge's manufacturers are understandably unhappy with the British results and believe their product to offer a better reliability rate than the 75-91 per cent figures recorded here. These figures include those women who might have used the sponge incorrectly, or not used it every time they had intercourse. It has been suggested that women who have had children might need a bigger size, but this is as yet unclear. The sponge could also be dislodged from the cervix during intercourse, though its absorbency and spermicide should mean that sperm will be killed before they can travel up through the cervical opening.

A higher chance of pregnancy may make the sponge unacceptable for you.

How to use a sponge

With the sponge in place you can have intercourse as often as you like for the next 24 hours without adding any extra spermicide. It is worth checking that it's still in place before you have intercourse again. You can insert the sponge well in advance of the time you have sex – as long as it's no longer than 24 hours beforehand.

You should remove the sponge not less than six hours after the last time you had intercourse. Put your finger inside your vagina and try to feel the loop attached to the sponge. Hook your finger round the loop and pull the sponge out of your vagina. This may be a bit tricky – often the sponge turns round inside the vagina so the loop is out of reach. And because the sponge is made of material that is meant to feel a a lot like the surface of the vagina you can be unsure of exactly what you are getting hold of. It will help if you bear down, as if you are having a bowel movement, so the sponge is pushed downwards in the vagina making it easier to reach.

Make sure you pull at the sponge very gently – it's important that it doesn't disintegrate inside the vagina. Removal of the sponge is a lot more difficult than insertion, and it may take a few times of using it before you work out the easiest way.

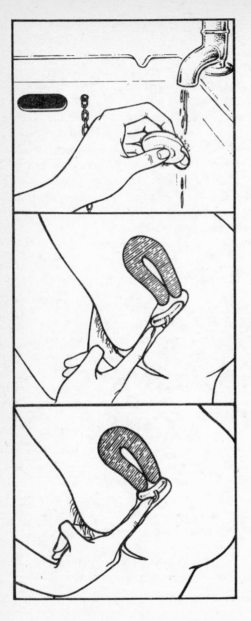

1 Moisten the sponge under a little running water, then squeeze it to release a little of the foamy spermicide.

2 Push the sponge up into your vagina with the indentation facing the cervix.

3 Push the sponge up and on to the cervix so the indentation is positioned directly over it, with the loop facing your fingers.

Once you have removed the sponge, simply throw it away (though not down the lavatory, as it floats and won't be flushed away properly).

The condom

Reliability rate 85-98 per cent

The condom is the only reversible contraceptive method for men — in other words, the only one that doesn't permanently affect fertility. It is about as reliable as the diaphragm or cap. If you use a spermicide as well you will be better protected if the sheath splits or falls off.

The condom is free from family planning clinics, though some have a rather strange rationing system. A recent survey found clinics giving clients an average of between three and 24 condoms a week, with no particular rationale for either amount. GPs don't prescribe condoms (see page 22). You can buy them at chemists, through mail order, or at barbers' shops.

There are various designs of condom, available in several colours. They all have teat ends, which hold the semen at ejaculation, but these may be of different design. Most are lubricated, and some are lubricated with a spermicide. You can also get special hypo-allergenic condoms if either you or your partner are allergic to rubber. Some condoms have a surface texture which is supposed to increase sexual pleasure for women. Since these textures are hardly discernible, and placed to touch parts of the vagina which have few if any nerve endings, this claim seems pretty unlikely. Condoms can be bought in packets of three, ten or twelve.

Condoms are almost as frequently used as the pill in this country, but there are still many men who dislike the idea of using them. They tend to be those who have become sexually active since the introduction of the pill, and whose only experience of condoms is associated with unconfident first-time sex. AIDS should change this (see page 63).

Types of condom

Brand Name	Design
SPERMICIDE-LUBRICATED CONDOMS:	
Durex Nu-Form Extra Safe	Teat end. Pink. Spermicide is nonoxynol 9
Elite	Teat end. Spermicide is nonoxynol 9
Ultrasure	Teat end. Spermicide is nonoxynol 9
LUBRICATED CONDOMS:	
Atlas	Teat end
Bon Accord	Teat end. Spermicide pessary provided for women
Durex allergy	Teat end. Hypo-allergenic
Durex Arouser	Teat end. Pink
Durex Black Shadow	Teat end. Black
Durex Fetherlite Extra Fine	Teat end
Durex Fiesta	Teat end. Variety of colours
Durex Gossamer	Teat end
Forget-me-not	Teat end
Lambutt Ideal	Teat end. Pink
Lambutt Safetex	Teat end
Lambutt Tru-shape	Shaped teat end
Nuda	Teat end
Tahiti	Shaped teat end. Three colours
Two's Company	Teat end. Spermicide pessary provided for woman
NON-LUBRICATED CONDOM	
Durex Dry	Can be used if either partner has allergy to spermicide, with KY jelly as lubricant instead. Also useful for semen collection for analysis in fertility investigation etc.

A number of imported condoms are also available – some from America, some from Europe. I have not listed them here as they have not undergone the standard British testing procedures as have the brands above.

How to use a condom

The condom should be carefully rolled onto the erect penis, making sure there is room left at the tip for the semen when the man has an orgasm. The end of the condom should be squeezed lightly between thumb and forefinger as it is rolled on. This minimizes the risk of the condom splitting.

You can use a spermicide at the same time – either a cream or jelly inserted with an applicator, a pessary or some foam. All the spermicides listed on page 66 can be used, and you can also use Genoxol (pH 5.0-7.5) or Rendells (pH 5.00-7.5). Both of these contain Nonoxynol 10 and 11.

After he has come, and before he loses his erection, your partner should hold on to the condom and withdraw his penis. This careful withdrawal should ensure that no semen is spilt into your vagina. Before throwing away the condom he should check it's not leaking or torn. A clear advantage of the condom is the fact that failure is likely to be more obvious, which means you could seek post-coital contraception (see page 140) if you wish. You should avoid close genital contact after he's taken off the condom, as he may well still have some semen on his penis.

Spermicides used on their own

Reliability rate 75-96 per cent

A variety of spermicides are available for use on their own. As well as those designed for use with barriers, others are marketed for use without any additional method. These are available as foam, pessaries and as a dissolvable film.

Use of a spermicide on its own is always discouraged by doctors and family planners. Research on effectiveness produces wildly differing results – sometimes as good as a diaphragm, sometimes far less good. Some forms of spermicide seem to be more effective than others. The film impregnated with spermicide had a high failure rate in a British trial. Foam appears to be the most reliable choice of spermicide, probably because it distributes itself in the vagina more effectively, and is more dense. There is clearly a high risk of pregnancy with spermicides used on their own – don't rely on them if it's vital that you don't get pregnant.

How to use a spermicide on its own

The recommended amount of spermicide (according to the instructions on the pack) should be placed high in the vagina and over the cervix. Pessaries can be inserted with your fingers. Cream, jelly and foam need an applicator.

The pack instructions will also tell you how long to wait until the spermicide is properly dissolved and distributed in the vagina. This could be anything from three to thirty minutes. The spermicide is likely to be active for around two hours, though some reduce in effectiveness after about twenty minutes. If you have intercourse more than once during the time specified on the pack, you'll need more spermicide.

The spermicide should be left in the vagina for at least six hours after intercourse. Do not douche or wash inside the vagina during this time. A bath may wash away spermicide too, so have a shower instead if you can.

Barriers and spermicides – effects on health

● **Cystitis**. You are more likely to develop cystitis if you use a diaphragm. This can be caused by the diaphragm pressing on the urethra (the tube leading from the bladder), causing irritation or bruising, or preventing complete emptying of the bladder. Cystitis could also be caused by the transfer of bacteria from the anus and rectum to the vagina, so it's important to have clean hands, genitals and anus before putting in the diaphragm. Both you and your partner should wash before making love.

You should also pee after sex, which will help wash away any bacteria transferred to the urethral opening. Some people suggest you should pee again ten minutes later to be doubly sure. It's a self-help method that does work, though it's tedious to have to get up twice in ten minutes to go to the lavatory. Cystitis sufferers should do this after sex whether or not they use a diaphragm. If you've never had cystitis you probably can't be bothered to pee twice, but once certainly is worth it.

If this is of no help, check back with your doctor or nurse that your diaphragm is the right size. If it is too big it may be causing undue pressure on the urethra. Even if the diaphragm is the right size, a change of rim design might be the answer. A softer rimmed design, like the coil spring, often suits women prone to cystitis better than the flat or arcing spring. A change to a less acid spermicide could also help (see page 66).

Don't leave the diaphragm in for too long. If you get cystitis, try to remove the diaphragm after six hours. If none of this works you may have to consider using a different barrier method, either a cap or a condom. If you still get cystitis it may be nothing to do with your method of contraception.

● **Toxic shock syndrome**. TSS is a serious, sometimes fatal, condition which causes a high temperature, sickness and diarrhoea, low blood pressure and shock. Although an increase in the bacteria which cause TSS has been found in barrier users, research has not revealed any increase in the chance of getting TSS itself if you use a barrier. The message is that you shouldn't leave the cap, diaphragm or sponge inside you for too long, just as tampon users are now being told to change tampons more frequently. And don't use a barrier during your period (this used to be suggested as a way of making intercourse less bloody when you were menstruating).

● **Spermicides and pregnancy**. If you do get accidentally pregnant while using a spermicide, could the pregnancy be affected? There has been a worry that sperm could be damaged by spermicide, but still be able to fertilise an egg. Some studies suggested a higher rate of Down's syndrome and other congenital abnormalities in babies born to women who got pregnant while using spermicides, as well as a higher rate of miscarriage. But recent research has been very reassuring – one large-scale American study involving 34,660 women found no evidence that the foetus was put at risk by exposure to spermicide at the time of conception.

● **The effect of spermicide on the rest of the body**. This is claimed to be minimal, but more research is needed before we can be sure. Earlier products, with a proven adverse effect, were withdrawn.

There is no clear evidence that spermicidal ingredients might be absorbed into the bloodstream, and if they are, what the effects might be. Experiments on animals have shown that spermicide can be present in the internal organs, and have also revealed spermicide in breast milk. It is not known what implications this has for women and children, if any. There has also been a suggestion that the sponge could contain carcinogens (cancer-causing chemicals), but this remains unconfirmed.

● **Allergy**. This could be to rubber or to spermicide, and could happen to you or your sexual partner. A sensation of burning or irritation in your vagina or on your partner's penis could indicate an allergy, as could cystitis-like symptoms in either of you. You might have an intolerance to the chemical make-up of the spermicide, so a change of brand might help. If you are allergic to rubber the alternatives are limited. Non-allergenic condoms are the only answer.

● **Protective effects of barriers**. Barriers almost certainly offer considerable protection against sexually transmitted disease (STD). These include the sexually transmitted herpes and papilloma viruses which are thought to be related to the later development of cervical cancer. Because you are less likely to get an STD with a barrier, you are also less likely to get the pelvic inflammatory disease (PID) which can sometimes follow, resulting in permanent damage and loss of fertility.

Barriers provide the cervix and penis with physical protection, and spermicides actually kill some STD organisms – especially gonorrhea, genital herpes, trichomonas and thrush. It has been confirmed in research that barrier users are less likely to get these, and are also less likely to get cervical cancer or the conditions that lead to it. This is a major advantage of barrier methods, and one which is beginning to get more publicity.

The condom provides considerable protection against Human Immunodeficiency Virus (HIV) which can lead to AIDS. As yet there has been no research showing whether some condoms are better than others in stopping the transmission of HIV, but all the British manufacturers claim that their products are strong enough to do so. Since HIV is contained in semen it is vital that none is spilt when the man withdraws his penis.

The spermicide Nonoxynol 9, contained in many brands (see page 66), has been found to kill HIV in laboratory conditions. It does this in very small concentrations, so although it has not yet been confirmed whether it would have the same effect in your vagina, it is definitely worth using both a spermicide and condom if you think either of you might be at risk.

● **Internal pain or bruising**. This could happen if the diaphragm is too big, or if you need one with a softer rim (see page 65). Rapid and deep intercourse could dislodge the cap or diaphragm, as can particular intercourse positions.

This has obvious implications for the contraceptive's reliability, so it's worth checking the device is in place after intercourse. Pain after or during sex could be caused by incorrect insertion of the device. However, it could have nothing to do with contraception, and might be an indication of pelvic infection, caused by something else. If you ever experience pain during sex you should see your doctor and get checked out.

Barriers – more research needed

Some women believe that barrier methods are free from all health risks, and that they should be promoted as such. Whilst it is clear that their side-effects are limited in comparison with other contraceptive methods, the health implications have not yet been fully researched. We need much more information on both their positive and negative effects on women's health.

Throughout this section I have talked about the gaps in knowledge about barrier methods. It is outrageous that this century's original contraceptive method needs more basic research, particularly at a time when more and more women are keen to stop using methods which do carry known risks to health.

No one is sure whether spermicides are actually needed, or in what quantity or circumstances, or how long they last. The effects on the body are still not clear. It is not surprising that manufacturers are less keen to develop methods that currently yield lower profits, but even independent medical researchers have been slow in responding to the need for reliable and acceptable new barrier methods.

Perhaps more important is that much of the positive information that *does* exist about barriers and spermicides is not adequately publicised. The methods have an important role in preventing sexually transmitted disease, the conditions which could lead to cervical cancer and AIDS. Such evidence could be a vital part of the decision to use a barrier, but instead we are told to limit the number of men we have sex with, or that if we suffer from these conditions we are somehow to blame. We need to know much more about this aspect of barriers, and have the opportunity to reduce the risk of illness by increasing our knowledge, not our fear.

7

FERTILITY AWARENESS

A commitment to self-knowledge and autonomy has been fundamental in the move away from conventional medicine and towards self-help made by many women in the last twenty years. It is therefore not surprising that there has been a renewed interest in fertility awareness as a way of avoiding pregnancy. No pills, no plastic, bits of wire or chemical jellies, just you and your sense of yourself reclaimed from the medical profession and big business.

Known in the past as the rhythm or the safe period method, fertility awareness is now being promoted as 'natural' family planning, with natural used in its modern (advertising-based?) sense to mean *good*. The obvious implication is that mechanical contraception is unnatural, and therefore *bad*. But any wish to avoid pregnancy involves, to some extent, an intervention in what is natural. Women have the physical potential for a natural reproductive life starting in our early teens and involving many pregnancies. When we decide not to fulfil that biological potential it could be argued that we are choosing the unnatural option. But it is a positive choice, and brings us many benefits — most notably that same autonomy which has led to an interest in fertility awareness.

Fertility awareness seems to me to be the most accurate and least prescriptive term for these methods. It means finding out when you are fertile, and making a decision about what you are going to do about it during that time. Those who don't want to use contraception at any time may decide to stop having sex altogether during the fertile days, but others may feel that abstaining from intercourse doesn't mean abstaining from sex. Oral sex and touching with your hands don't result in pregnancy at any time of the cycle. If you want to have intercourse during the fertile days you could use fertility awareness methods in conjunction with barriers and spermicide. So fertility awareness does not have to involve 'periodic abstinence' as its detractors like to say.

Many women assume that the physical safety of fertility awareness methods is their major advantage, but this means you're looking at only one aspect of using the methods. They certainly don't do any harm, but they are much more likely to result in pregnancy than is mechanical contraception. In choosing to use these methods you may be taking on a greater risk of pregnancy and the physical risks it can involve.

Fertility awareness methods are the only form of contraception approved by the Roman Catholic Church, which means they are the only acceptable methods for some women. But there may be other reasons – cultural and medical – why you want to use them. Roman Catholic organisations, which are very keen to teach the methods, may be the best place to learn regardless of your religion. A few NHS family planning clinics will provide a teacher.

Good teaching is vital if you are to use these methods with confidence, and if they are to be reliable. This section on fertility awareness is intended to be an introduction to the methods you can use, and to give you some idea of what will be involved if you decide to use them. You'll need detailed and personal teaching if you think any of the methods will suit you. This is likely to involve six sessions lasting about an hour each. You'll almost certainly be invited to bring your partner along too. Even if he is unable to do this you will need his cooperation and support if you are to feel good about using the method, and he will need to understand and accept the basic principles of whatever fertility awareness method you choose.

What is fertility awareness?

Your body goes through a series of changes throughout the menstrual cycle. These are triggered by hormone changes. Some are noticeable, some are not. Fertility awareness methods involve finding out what is happening to your body from day to day, and working out, with the help of this information, when you are ovulating and therefore likely to get pregnant. Women who want to get pregnant can also use fertility awareness, especially through observing changes in cervical mucus. Temperature charts are less useful, as they only give you information in retrospect – you know that you have ovulated, but it's more difficult to tell when you are going to. If you want to get pregnant it's best to have intercourse just before ovulation, so that sperm will be ready and waiting to fertilise the egg at the moment it is released.

You will need to become used to charting these changes for several cycles – most teachers say six – before relying on fertility awareness as a way of avoiding pregnancy. During this time you can get an idea of how the cycle is affected by factors like stress or travel, and you'll also have a chance to compare records covering a number of months and identify what are the consistent signs of ovulation.

Although you are fertile for only 24-48 hours in each cycle, you will see that each of the methods described involves not having intercourse for a number of days. This is because sperm remain able to fertilise an egg for around three to five days inside you – maybe as many as seven days. So you could become pregnant as a result of the intercourse you had last week, even though you are ovulating only now.

It may be more difficult for you to calculate ovulation in advance if your periods are very irregular. But even if the amount of time between periods varies considerably, the time between ovulation and menstruation does not. It is always between 11-16 days. If you are clear on what your own signs of ovulation are the cycle length shouldn't matter. There are certain times in your life when your cycle is likely to be irregular, which could make it more difficult to predict your cyclical pattern. Young women whose cycle has yet to be established may also find it more difficult, as may older women who are beginning to experience the menopause. It could take some time after childbirth before your cycle is regular again, but if you are already knowledgeable about your own signs of ovulation you should still be able to recognise them.

All the methods require a considerable amount of record-keeping and organisation, and you will need to feel positive about fertility awareness if it is not to become a chore. You may also find the experience considerably more enjoyable if you have the support and interest of your sexual partner. At the very least he should be prepared to accept without argument that there will be times in the month when you won't be able to have intercourse without contraception, or perhaps any intercourse at all. But women whose partners are involved in the day-to-day experience of fertility awareness do say it has benefited their relationships. It can also promote sexual enjoyment, because sexual activity is not limited to intercourse alone.

Autonomy – the personal control you have over your fertility – is one of the greatest advantages of these methods. Once you have learned how to chart your own menstrual cycle, no further follow-up or involvement with teachers or doctors is needed. If you want to use the methods to help you get pregnant you can, and there's no need to return for further consultations.

The calendar method

This method entirely relies on a record of the length of your menstrual cycle, kept for at least six months beforehand. You need to know the number of days in each cycle during that time – how many days there are between the first days of each period. Very few women have the textbook 28-day cycle.

Over six months you may arrive at a series of figures like this:

$$28-28-31-30-28-33$$

These provide the basis of calculations to discover your fertile time. You need to leave a margin of a few days to include the possibility of sperm survival and your own changes in ovulation time from cycle to cycle. It's done (using the figures above) like this:

> subtract 20 from the shortest cycle length to find your *first* fertile day: $28-20=8$
> subtract 10 from the longest cycle length to find your *last* fertile day: $33-10=23$

You then mark up a calendar accordingly:

Here is the chart showing the first unsafe day (day 8, which is the 10th of the calendar month) and the last unsafe day (day

Monday		⑤	✗	✗	26
Tuesday		⑥	✗	✗	27
Wednesday		⑦	✗	✗	28
Thursday	1	8	✗	✗	29
Friday	2	9	✗	✗	30
Saturday	③	✗	✗	✗	㉛
Sunday	④	✗	✗	✗	

O = period

x = days you can't have intercourse

23, which is the 25th of the calendar month). You would therefore be able to have intercourse without contraception on 12 days (the uncrossed ones) of this particular cycle, which this month has lasted for 28 days.

A shorter menstrual cycle will mean fewer days each month during which you can have intercourse without contraception. A longer cycle would mean there would be more days. You'll need to maintain your records of your cycle, and amend your calculations if it gets longer or shorter.

The calendar method used on its own is not very reliable – it is estimated at only around 53 per cent sure. This is partly because many couples do not choose to stop intercourse for the whole of the possibly fertile time, and partly because cycle lengths and ovulation times may change from month to month. This is partly because it involves such a long time without intercourse, and partly because cycle lengths and ovulation times may change from month to month. None of those who teach fertility awareness would be likely to recommend it as a single indicator of fertility.

The temperature method

This method relies on changes in body temperature during the menstrual cycle. After ovulation the temperature rises a little (between 0.2 and 0.4 degrees Celsius) and stays at this raised level until the beginning of the next period. Once the temperature has remained at this higher level for three days you can have intercourse without contraception, up until your period starts.

You cannot have intercourse without contraception from the day your period starts until after ovulation and the three days of consistently higher temperature readings.

It helps to have a special ovulation thermometer, called a Zeal thermometer, for these readings, on which it is easier to read the small changes you have to record. A change as small as 0.1 of a degree is clear on a Zeal thermometer. It's available from family planning clinics or on prescription from your GP. An ordinary thermometer is okay, but is more difficult to read.

● **Take your temperature daily on waking and before getting up** because any activity is likely to raise the temperature slightly. You must not eat or drink anything until you've taken your temperature.

● **Leave the thermometer in your mouth for five minutes**. You could, if you prefer, take your temperature by putting the thermometer in your vagina or rectum, in which case three minutes will be enough. But always use the same part of your body to take these readings, as alternating might confuse the results.

● **Record your daily temperature on a special chart** available from family planning clinics and fertility awareness teachers. These charts tend to be fiddly and small, so if you have a disability which affects your sight, manual dexterity or coordination your partner could note the changes for you. Or you could ask him or a friend to draw up a larger-scale chart on which you could record the readings yourself. Commercially marketed recorders (which cost around £40) are also available, which do the calculating for you.

● **Your temperature might change for reasons other than ovulation**, like a cold, a late night, alcohol the night before, or because of drugs you might be taking. Aspirin, for instance, lowers the temperature. You should record all these factors as well as taking your daily temperature, so that you are better able to tell which are the temperature changes that signify ovulation.

The reliability of the temperature method is greater than that of the calendar method – it is likely to be upwards of 80-85 per cent. If

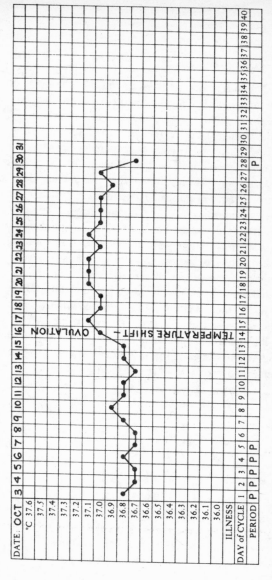

Temperature chart showing 10 safe days in the 28 day cycle

you stick to the rule about not having intercourse until three days after ovulation the reliability rate is 94 per cent.

The cervical mucus method

Ovulation is accompanied by a number of changes which encourage fertilisation of the egg. The cervix opens a little, and produces mucus which is wetter and easier for sperm to travel through. At other times during the cycle the mucus is thicker and drier, and keeps sperm away from the uterus and fallopian tubes.

The cervical mucus method involved charting these changes, and working out on which days of the cycle you are likely to be fertile. Once again, you must allow time for the survival of sperm, and allow a wide margin of time for reliability.

Cervical mucus changes in its appearance and also how it makes your vagina feel during the cycle. Following your period you'll feel particularly dry, because you are likely to have a plug of mucus in the cervix. Immediately after this slightly wetter mucus will appear – it will be thick or sticky, and a kind of cloudy white colour.

Just before and during ovulation the mucus becomes clear, wet and slippery, and there's a lot more of it. You'll have a sensation of wetness in the vagina, and there could be a slight mid-cycle bleed. This mucus will be stretchy and form into strands if you hold it between your thumb and forefinger, unlike the stickier non-fertile mucus.

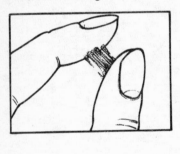

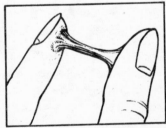

After the ovulatory wetness the mucus will become drier and sticker again and will go back to its cloudy white look.

How to use the cervical mucus method

You should examine your mucus at a convenient time every day – perhaps before you have a bath or when you go to the toilet. You can either put your finger into your vagina and examine the mucus that covers the finger, or wipe a tissue across your vaginal opening and examine that.

You can have intercourse without contraception during the dry days immediately following your period, but must cease as soon as you have any sensation of wetness. Continue to abstain from intercourse without contraception throughout the days of peak wetness and beyond, until you have had four dry days in succession. Then you can have intercourse without contraception.

You'll need to record these changes throughout the cycle on a special chart which you can draw up yourself or get from a fertility awareness teacher. A 28-day cycle could look like the one on page 94. This cycle shows there is a total of 12 dry days in the cycle when you could have intercourse without contraception. Some teachers suggest you should have intercourse only on *alternate* days immediately after your period, as the semen that may still be in your vagina can be confusing and produce inaccurate readings. You can start having intercourse without contraception on the evening of the fourth dry day after the ovulatory wetness.

If you do have sex *with contraception* during the wet days it may make it difficult to tell what's happening to your cervical mucus. Spermicide, for example, may make your vagina quite wet for hours or more afterwards. A vaginal infection like thrush or trichomonas may also be confusing particularly if it happens mid-cycle, and may make it impossible to know whether or not you are ovulating.

The cervical mucus method is a great deal more reliable than the calendar method, but opinions about its effectiveness vary considerably. There have been claims that it is 98 per cent reliable, but most research puts its reliability at 80-85 per cent. But this figure includes those who may have had intercourse without contraception during the wet days.

| PEAK FERTILITY | MUCUS | | PERIOD/SPOTTING | DAY of CYCLE |
	APPEARANCE	SENSATION		
			P	1
			P	2
			P	3
			P	4
			P	5
		DRY		6
		DRY		7
		DRY		8
X	THICK	MOIST		9
X	THICK	MOIST		10
X	STRETCHY	WET		11
X	STRETCHY	WET		12
X	STRETCHY	WET		13
X	THICK	MOIST		14
		DRY		15
				16
				17
				18
				19
				20
				21
				22
				23
				24
				25
				26
				27
			P	28
				29
				30
				31
				32
				33
				34
				35
				36
				37
				38
				39
				40

Chart showing sensation and appearance recorded on each day

Fertility detection kits

There is now a range of commercially marketed kits which measure changes in your urine which show when you are ovulating. They cost around £30, and require you to do between 7-10 tests every cycle. Because these kits can't predict ovulation they are more suitable for when you are trying to get pregnant than when you want to avoid conception. They could be useful if you wanted to combine the technique with other fertility awareness methods.

Combining fertility awareness methods

The **symptothermal method** combines the cervical mucus and the temperature methods, as well as incorporating other signs of physical changes through the menstrual cycle. You can enter your own personal changes into the recording of your cycle to produce a more subjective and accurate assessment of your fertile and non-fertile days.

The cervix changes through the menstrual cycle, becoming softer and having an enlarged opening during ovulation. Its position may change too. Over a series of cycles you can become familiar with these changes by doing a daily self-examination. Your breasts may become tender and uncomfortable in the days leading up to a period, and you may have other symptoms that you associate with the pre-menstrual phase. Some women have an ovulation pain (called *Mittelschmerz*, which is German for middle-pain) in the middle of the cycle. Others have a little mid-cycle bleed at this time. Both of these can act as confirmation of the other changes you have noticed, like the arrival of fertile mucus.

Not surprisingly, combining methods produces the greatest reliability rate of all fertility awareness methods (85-93 per cent). You'll need to feel committed to this approach, and be interested in learning more about your body. Once you are confident that you can recognise the cyclical changes the method won't take up so much time, but it will take a good few months before you have a clear picture of all the changes that happen. It's useful to have a good teacher whom you can trust over this time, who can show you

Chart showing the symptothermal method

DATE: OCTOBER		3	4	5	6	7	8	9	10	11	12	13	14	15	16	17	18
	°C 37.6																
	37.5														OVULATION		
	37.4																
	37.3																
	37.2																
	37.1															●	
	37.0																●
	36.9							●									
	36.8	●			●			●	●	●			●	●			
	36.7		●	●		●	●				●						
	36.6																
	36.5														TEMPERATURE SHIFT –		
	36.4																
	36.3																
	36.2																
	36.1																
	36.0																
DAY of CYCLE		1	2	3	4	5	6	7	8	9	10	11	12	13	14	15	1
PERIOD/SPOTTING		P	P	P	P	P											
MUCUS	SENSATION						DRY	DRY	DRY	MOIST	MOIST	WET	WET	WET	MOIST	DRY	
	APPEARANCE									THICK	THICK	STRETCHY	STRETCHY	STRETCHY	THICK		
PAIN																	
BREAST TENDERNESS																	
ILLNESS																	
FERTILE DAYS										F	F	F	F	F	F	F	F
SEXUAL INTERCOURSE					✓	✓		✓									

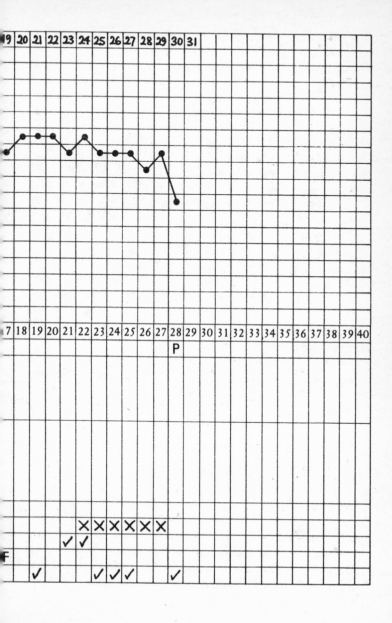

exactly what to do. Record-keeping is vital, otherwise you'll have no way of comparing what happens from cycle to cycle.

Pregnancy and fertility awareness methods

For a variety of reasons, fertility awareness methods are less reliable than most other forms of contraception. Many women who use the methods do so in order to 'space' the number of children they have, and don't feel that an unplanned pregnancy would be a disaster. If you definitely want to avoid pregnancy you would probably feel more confident using mechanical contraception – either throughout the cycle or on the days when pregnancy is likely (see below).

There have been worrying reports in recent years about an increase in congenital abnormality (both physical and mental) and miscarriage in pregnancies conceived by women while using fertility awareness methods. This was thought to be due to abnormality caused by an *aged sperm* (perhaps one that has been inside you for three days or more) fertilising the egg. Another theory was that it could be caused by an *aged egg* that remains ready to be fertilised for some time after the end of what the couple thinks is the fertile time. The ageing of both sperm and egg has been thought to result in chromosomal abnormality.

Though a few research studies have indicated this problem, subsequent studies have not shown any increased risk of abnormality. But it still remains a possibility, despite these recent and reassuring results.

Combining fertility awareness with contraception

If you have no objection to using contraception, but want to keep its use to a minimum, then combining it with fertility awareness can be a good option. It means using a barrier method (diaphragm, cap, sponge or condom) because the pill and IUD have to be used all the time.

This approach is not promoted much, probably because it is so much within women's control, rather than in the control of the medical profession. Many doctors are resistant to the idea of self-help and self-knowledge, believing that medical amateurs (women) can't know enough about physiology to be able to understand the changes that happen in their own bodies during the menstrual cycle, and decide for themselves when they are likely to be fertile. Many women who use barrier methods probably use a variation on fertility awareness as well – maybe not using contraception immediately before a period – but don't mention this to their doctors, as they know they are likely to get a disapproving response. It appears that no research has been done on the reliability rates of combining fertility awareness methods with barrier contraception.

How you decide to do it is a matter of personal preference. You could choose the symptothermal method, and use a diaphragm and spermicide through the beginning and middle of the cycle, and then have intercourse without the barrier once you get symptoms of the pre-menstrual phase – tender breasts, for instance. Or you could have intercourse without contraception up until you notice fertile mucus, and then use contraception until you have had the four 'dry' days.

The major difficulty in doing this is that the presence of both semen and spermicide in your vagina can mean that it's difficult to know when the dry days have started. It will be easier if your partner uses a condom, because there won't be any semen in the vagina. But the vaginal wetness of sexual arousal could still be confusing.

If you don't have any pronounced premenstrual symptoms you won't know whether you need contraception or not. But the more you get to know about your cycle and its pattern of physical changes, the more likely it is that you will be able to work out for yourself what's happening at any particular time within it. Comprehensive record-keeping should help you here.

Remember that it's the time *running up to ovulation* that is the most difficult to predict. The time you ovulate may change from cycle to cycle, with a shift of a few days making all the difference to reliability. But once you have ovulated the signs should be more clear, and can then be relied upon.

And even if you would rather not have intercourse during the fertile days, remember that this does not mean abstinence from sex itself, only from one specific sexual act: intercourse.

(Note: **Astrological birth control** (also known as **Lunarception**) is based on the idea that you are fertile when the sun and moon are in the same position as they were when you were born. You would have to avoid intercourse at both this time and the time you have calculated as your fertile time using one of the methods above. I have no evidence that this method works, so have not included it in this section.)

8

WITHDRAWAL
Coitus Interruptus

The withdrawal method has probably been used as a way of avoiding pregnancy since the moment it was realised that pregnancy was associated with intercourse and ejaculation of semen. It is certainly still used by millions of couples around the world, despite the advent of contraceptives that stop pregnancy even though semen is present.

The method is very simple – all it means is that your partner doesn't come inside you, but withdraws his penis from your vagina just before he has an orgasm, and then comes.

Withdrawal has not been promoted at all by family planning organisations, mainly because of the belief that it is very unreliable. The theory is that sperm are contained in the pre-orgasmic fluid that comes from the penis when the man is very aroused, so that you could get pregnant even if the actual orgasm that follows happens when he has withdrawn.

But the evidence for this turns out to be very slight. If your partner has not had an orgasm for some days there may be no sperm left in the penis which could then get into the pre-orgasmic fluid. Even if they are present, there are likely to be very few, compared to the many millions there are in an average orgasmic ejaculation of semen, and probably not enough to fertilise an egg. So if your partner is vigilant about withdrawing before orgasm you may be very unlikely to get pregnant.

Studies done in the past into the method's effectiveness have shown quite good reliability rates – between 80 and 95 per cent –

which, though not as good as mechanical contraceptives, are not that different from the reliability of fertility awareness methods, and a great deal more reliable than not using a contraceptive at all. And of course there are no other effects on the body, like those caused by methods such as the pill or the IUD.

Those who are against the method say that it can cause psychosexual problems. The man may become so preoccupied with the moment of orgasm that he could develop orgasm difficulties like premature ejaculation, which in turn is likely to make the method unreliable, or he may simply find it less sexually satisfying than coming inside you. They also suggest that it will be frustrating sexually for the woman, though it is difficult to see why this would be true for withdrawal more than any other method. If your partner comes before you it doesn't much matter whether he comes when he's withdrawn, into a condom or inside your pill-protected body – you could find it sexually frustrating anyway if continued intercourse is what you want. And, regardless of what kind of contraception you are using, if he comes before you do it's still possible for you to have an orgasm with oral sex, or with masturbation done by you or by him.

The withdrawal method's single modern champion is Germaine Greer. Writing in her book *Sex and Destiny* she promotes it as a positive male contraceptive method which can free women from 'horrible and dangerous experiences with contraceptive hardware and steroids'. What she fails to confront is the fact that control over the withdrawal method lies entirely with the man, leaving the woman once more dependent on men's trustworthiness and reliability. And if there is one single corner of worry about whether or not he will 'be careful', sex for the woman is unlikely to be relaxed, positive and unselfconscious. This can be too high a price to pay for the freedom from mechanical contraceptives.

But even so, withdrawal may still be worth considering, especially if you can accept the possibility of a higher chance of pregnancy. You may not do it every time you have intercourse, or may choose to combine it with fertility awareness methods. What's important is that both you and your partner are confident that he will withdraw in time, and that neither of you minds him not having an orgasm inside you.

9

HORMONAL METHODS

More than fifty million women worldwide take the contraceptive pill. For over a quarter of a century it has been the most reliable and popular method of reversible contraception, as well as a crucial component in the major change in attitudes about women, reproduction and sexuality.

A range of other hormone-based contraceptives has been developed following the originally marketed pill, all of which prevent pregnancy in a similar way, but are delivered into the body differently. Long-lasting injections, hormone-releasing vaginal rings and slow release implants have all been developed to be used by women who for one reason or another can't use the contraceptive pill. And it's now possible to obtain hormonal contraception *after* sex when, for instance, a sheath has broken or no contraception has been used.

A quarter of a century on from the first generally available pills, the current versions are somewhat more sophisticated. Lower doses of synthetic hormones are used, with a resultant decrease in bad effects on health. More is known about other factors that may increase the risk of bad effects, and there is more known about who should and shouldn't use this method.

Those who take the pill probably know more about it than any other drug they take, but since few of us are biochemists our understanding is bound to be limited to a pretty simple understanding of what it is and what it does. We are dependent on the popular press for information about research studies and their findings, much of which is presented as sensational pill-scare stories. And whilst it is true that the pill is the most researched drug in the world, there are still many unanswered questions surrounding it.

Suggestions that the pill could be linked to the later development of cancer got considerable publicity a few years ago, but remain unproven. Equally, no one has been able to prove that these drugs *don't* cause cancer. And no one knows what the long-term effects are, either on us, our children, or grandchildren and beyond.

The major advantage of hormonal contraception is its reliability in preventing pregnancy and its non-intervention in sex. For many women the known and unknown health risks are outweighed by these two factors. And it's true that using the method has enabled millions of women to explore and assert their sexuality without risking pregnancy. Many of those who now favour and propagandise the use of barrier methods developed an important sexual confidence through using the pill, and perhaps would not have been half as positive and assertive without it.

But to a great extent this was done in ignorance of what the physical effects of the pill might be. It wasn't until the late 1970s that the nature of the combination pill's link with an increased risk of circulatory disease became clear, prompting an estimated one million women in this country to stop using it. The long-term effects of the pill, particularly the risk of cancer, are still unclear.

Now many women are questioning the nature of the 'freedom' provided by the pill, suggesting that it makes us free to engage in a kind of sexuality defined by men, and not by ourselves. The existence of the pill has contributed to the tyranny of the belief that the only *real* sex is intercourse, and that any other kind of sex is just a step on the way to the real thing. The pill may increase our sexual availability to men, but that does not mean we are any more liberated.

With the development of better and more reliable barrier methods, as well as reversible methods of sterilisation and new types of contraceptive drugs, the days of the hormonal contraceptive look numbered. But for the time being it remains the method most frequently used in this country.

The following two pages show the natural hormonal activity of a normal menstrual cycle, and set out the changes caused by the combined pill.

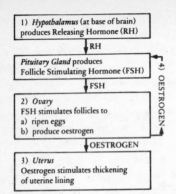

Days 1-14 of a 28 day menstrual cycle

1) Releasing Hormone (RH) is sent from the brain to the pituitary gland, which then produces follicle stimulating hormone (FSH).

2) FSH is sent to the ovaries where it causes eggs to ripen in the follicles. At the same time the follicles produce oestrogen. This has two effects on the cycle ...

3) Oestrogen stimulates the growth of the uterine lining in readiness for a fertilised egg.

4) Oestrogen slows down the release of FSH from the pituitary.

During this 'follicular phase' of the cycle the eggs are ripened in the ovary. The oestrogen gradually reduces the amount of FSH from the pituitary. At about day 14 the oestrogen reaches such a level that it triggers the release of Luteinising Hormone (LH) from the pituitary.

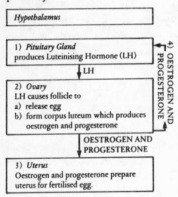

Days 14-28 of a 28 day menstrual cycle

1) Luteinising Hormone (LH) goes from pituitary to ovary.

2) LH causes the follicle with the ripest egg to release it into fallopian tube where it can be fertilised. That follicle then produces both oestrogen and progesterone.

3) Oestrogen and progesterone stimulate preparation of uterus for pregnancy, especially uterine lining which becomes thicker.

4) Oestrogen and progesterone are fed back to the pituitary gland. Oestrogen continues to inhibit the release of FSH and the increasing level of progesterone gradually slows down release of LH.

Twelve to fourteen days after the start of the luteal phase the corpus luteum stops producing oestrogen and progesterone. The fall in hormone level triggers the brain to produce more releasing hormone, which in turn begins a new cycle. The fall in hormone level also results in the shedding of the uterine lining – this is the menstrual period.

Fertilisation

* if an egg is fertilised it will be implanted about five days after release

* the embryo produces HCG, a hormone which acts like LH

* HCG enables the corpus luteum to keep producing oestrogen and progesterone

* this continued production of oestrogen and progesterone prevents shedding of uterine lining and protects embryo and prevents menstruation

* high levels of oestrogen and progesterone prevent release of FSH and LH

The combined pill

The pill contains oestrogen and progestogen (synthetic progesterone). It:

* reduces FSH and LH so no eggs mature or are released

* thickens cervical mucus so it acts as a barrier to sperm

* makes the uterine lining less hospitable to a fertilized egg

* slows down action of fallopian tubes in transporting an egg

During the 21 pill-taking days the uterine lining thickens slightly. During the 7 pill-free days the hormone level drops causing a 'withdrawal bleed'.

The combined pill

Reliability rate 99 per cent

The combined pill is the most popular of the hormonal methods. Its main effect is to stop ovulation, so that pregnancy is virtually impossible. During a normal menstrual cycle a number of different hormones are produced, which trigger the sequence that leads to the monthly releasing of an egg. The combined pill, with the two synthetic hormones oestrogen and progestogen, intervene in the sequence to stop the ovulation trigger that comes from the pituitary gland. In this way the pill mimics pregnancy. It's as if ovulation and fertilisation have already taken place, so there's no need for the pituitary gland to stimulate the production of another egg. The ovaries themselves are probably not directly inhibited by the pill – what they lack is the trigger to produce eggs.

The combined pill is usually taken daily for three weeks, followed by a seven-day break, during which a 'withdrawal bleed' takes place. This is a blood loss caused by the withdrawal of the hormones that have been maintaining the uterine lining during the three pill-taking weeks. This withdrawal bleed is not a period, and it is not necessarily vital that you should have it (see page 126). But it does act as confirmation that you are not pregnant, and means an overall reduction in the amount of hormones you take. It's also thought that women like to have a regular 'period' because that's what they're used to. This belief led to the earlier prescription of the pill as a way of supposedly regularising an unpredictable menstrual cycle – what it in fact did was impose a pill cycle in place of the menstrual one, and no long-term change could be expected once pill-taking ceased. There were other reasons too – see page 17.

The pill has other effects on the reproductive system apart from inhibiting ovulation. The lining of the uterus is changed in a way that makes it less likely to allow a fertilised egg to implant, in the unlikely event of 'breakthrough ovulation'. The mucus in the cervical opening is also changed, to make it more difficult for sperm to get through. It becomes more dense and difficult to penetrate.

The amount of oestrogen in the combined pill has been reduced over the years, and in the phased pills the progestogen has been reduced by as much as 30 per cent, leading the US magazine *Ms* recently to describe the pills that are currently on offer as 'the new pill'. But its basic action remains the same, even though the side-effects are less, particularly on the cardiovascular system. Most pills are described as low-dose these days – the only question is how low.

Your doctor should choose the lowest oestrogen dose to suit you from this list, and most women are put on the pills containing 30mg and under of oestrogen to start with. But you could find you need a higher dose of oestrogen – if you are on long-term medication that reduces the oestrogen's effectiveness (see page 118) or if you find you have breakthrough bleeding (see page 124).

All these pills differ in progestogen levels too, but it's impossible to make a genuinely meaningful chart out of these different levels, because the *amount* of progestogen does not necessarily define its

Combined pills containing 50 mg or less of oestrogen:

Brand name	Description	Type of oestrogen	Amount in mg
Anovlar 21	21 green pills	Ethinoestradiol	50
Eugynon 50	21 white pills	Ethinoestradiol	50
Gynovlar 21	21 pink pills	Ethinoestradiol	50
Minilyn	22 white pills	Ethinoestradiol	50
Minovlar	21 yellow pills	Ethinoestradiol	50
Minovlar ED	21 yellow pills and 7 dummy pills	Ethinoestradiol	50
Norinyl 1	21 white pills	Mestranol	50
Ortho-Novin 1/50	21 white pills	Mestranol	50
Ovran	21 white pills	Ethinoestradiol	50
Brevinor	21 white pills	Ethinoestradiol	35
Neocon 1/35	21 peach pills	Ethinoestradiol	35
Norimin	21 yellow pills	Ethinoestradiol	35
Ovysmen	21 white pills	Ethinoestradiol	35

Combined pills containing 30 mg or less of oestrogen:

Brand name	Description	Type of oestrogen	Amount in mg
Conova 30	21 white pills	Ethinoestradiol	30
Eugynon 30	21 white pills	Ethinoestradiol	30
Loestrin 30	21 green pills	Ethinoestradiol	30
Loestrin 20	21 blue pills	Ethinoestradiol	20
Marvelon	21 white pills	Ethinoestradiol	30
Microgynon 30	21 beige pills	Ethinoestradiol	30
Ovran 30	21 white pills	Ethinoestradiol	30
Ovranette	21 white pills	Ethinoestradiol	30

Phased combination pills:

Brand name	Description	Type of oestrogen	Amount in mg
Binovum	7 white pills	Ethinoestradiol	35
	14 peach pills	Ethinoestradiol	35
Logynon and	6 brown pills	Ethinoestradiol	30
Trinordiol	5 white pills	Ethinoestradiol	40
	10 yellow pills	Ethinoestradiol	50
Logynon ED	Exactly the same as Trinodiol and Logynon but with an extra 7 white dummy pills		
Trinovum	7 white pills	Ethinoestradiol	35
	7 peach pills	Ethinoestradiol	35
	7 dark peach pills	Ethinoestradiol	35
Synphase	7 white pills	Ethinoestradiol	0.035
	9 yellow pills	Ethinoestradiol	0.035
	5 white pills	Ethinoestradiol	0.035

strength. Some progestogens are more potent than others, so what looks like a smaller dose may in fact have a more powerful influence on your body. What counts in this chart is the type of progestogen – something you may consider if you need to change brands.

Progestogen content in combination pills:

Brand name	Progestogen type	Amount in mg
Anovlar 21	Norethisterone acetate	4.0
Brevinor	Norethisterone	0.5
Conova 30	Ethynodiol diacetate	2.0
Eugynon 30	Levonorgestrel	0.25
Eugynon 50	Norgestrel	0.25
Gynovlar 21	Norethisterone acetate	3.0
Loestrin 20	Norethisterone acetate	1.0
Loestrin 30	Norethisterone acetate	1.5
Marvelon	Desogestrel	0.15
Microgynon 30	Levonorgestrel	0.15
Minilyn	Lynoestrenol	2.5
Minovlar	Norethisterone acetate	1.0
Minovlar ED	Norethisterone acetate	1.0
Neocon 1/35	Norethisterone	1.0
Norimin	Norethisterone	1.0
Norinyl 1	Norethisterone	1.0
Ortho Novin 1/50	Norethisterone	1.0
Ovran	Levonorgestrel	0.25
Ovran 30	Levonorgestrel	0.25
Ovranette	Levonorgestrel	0.15
Ovysmen	Norethisterone	0.5

Phased pills reduce the amount of hormone you take overall. The graded dose of progestogen in the phased pill adds up to 30 per cent less than the amount of progestogen you would take during a month on a single phase combined pill. This phasing is meant to mimic the menstrual cycle – you'll see that the highest dose is in the middle of the month when you are most likely to ovulate. A phased pill is

Progestogen content in phased combination pills:

Brand name	Progestogen type	Amount in mg
Binovum	first 7 pills: Norethisterone	0.05
	next 14 pills: Norethisterone	1.00
Trinordiol and Logynon	first 6 pills: Levonorgestrel	0.05
	next 5 pills: Levonorgestrel	0.075
	next 10 pills: Levonorgestrel	0.125
Trinovum	first 7 pills: Norethisterone	0.05
	next 7 pills: Norethisterone	0.075
	last 7 pills: Norethisterone	1.0
Synphase	first 7 pills: Norethisterone	0.05
	next 9 pills: Norethisterone	1.0
	last 5 pills: Norethisterone	0.035

For brand names in Australia and New Zealand see page 211.

slightly less reliable than a monophasic pill. Some doctors prefer the monophasic pill because the margin for error is less – they worry that you might take pills from the wrong phase at the wrong time.

Before you take the pill

The pill is available only on prescription, so you'll need to see a doctor. The doctor should take your full medical history, as well as the medical history of your immediate family. A history of cardiovascular disease, especially of high blood pressure, in you or someone in your family when they were young, might mean the pill is unsuitable for you, as might a history of cancer of the breast or of the reproductive organs. The doctor will need to know whether you've had a recent pregnancy (ending in birth, miscarriage or abortion). Your current weight and blood pressure level should also be recorded. Even without a clear history of cardiovascular disease, there are many reasons why you may not be able to take the pill. You should not take it if you have or have had any of the following conditions, because it could increase the risk of developing cardiovascular disease:

● **Circulatory disease** including thrombosis, stroke, and a specific and rare sort of migraine called 'crescendo migraine' which increases the risk of a pill-related stroke.

● **Any condition which increases risk of thrombosis**, including severe diabetes, very high blood pressure, abnormally high chloresterol (fat) levels in the blood, or angina (pain in the heart caused by hardening of the arteries). Severe diabetes increases the risk of thrombosis as well, especially if it has already caused liver damage. There is also an increased risk of thrombosis if you are over 45, if you smoke, or are very overweight. Physical disability which means you are physically inactive for most of the time, either using a wheelchair or lying down a lot, also increases the risk. If you are due for a major operation (which in itself increases the risk of thrombosis) you should not start taking the pill. It is best not to take it for four weeks before and six weeks after the operation – this applies to those already on the pill too.

● **Varicose veins** are not in themselves a reason not to take the pill, unless they are accompanied by other factors which mean you shouldn't take it.

● **Sickle cell anaemia**, a rare kind of anaemia which affects Black people, is known to increase the risk of thrombosis. There is no evidence at the moment that you should definitely avoid the combination pill if you have sickle cell anaemia, but research into this is under way. You should consult your doctor, who may prefer to prescribe the progestogen-only pill (see page 133). **Sickle cell trait** does not carry the same risk of thrombosis, so in this case it is okay to take the pill.

Even if none of these apply to you, the pill may still not be suitable. Other conditions could be made worse by taking the pill, including:

● **Liver disease** (for instance hepatitis). You should not take the pill until liver function tests show you are recovered. Jaundice in pregnancy and cirrhosis of the liver are also contra-indications, as is a liver tumour.

● **A history of cancer**, either known or suspected, in the breast, cervix, ovary, uterus or vagina. Some doctors will not prescribe the pill if your mother or sister has had breast cancer, but others see this as over-cautious. Researchers are also undecided whether an abnormal cervical smear ranks as a contra-indication to taking the combined pill, but given this uncertainty it may be better to consider a different form of contraception until you have had a normal smear result. Many doctors will still prescribe the pill in these circumstances, as long as you are regularly monitored.

● **History of illness that happens or gets worse in pregnancy.** This means that the pill could trigger it once again, because of the similar hormones that are involved. This is why you should not take it if you have had jaundice during pregnancy (see above), or if you have severe diabetes. There are other diseases which are known sometimes to get worse in pregnancy, such as multiple sclerosis (MS) and Hodgkin's disease, but there is no evidence at this point that the pill has the same effect. If you have any disorder of the immune system (such as MS) you should discuss this with the doctor who is prescribing the pill.

● **Lack of periods (amenorrhoea) or irregular bleeding from your vagina for which the cause is not known.** These should be investigated before you are prescribed the pill. It may turn out that it is okay to take it once the cause has been discovered and you've had any necessary treatment.

Therefore, **if you've only just started menstruating** and your periods are not yet regular, you will probably have to wait before starting the pill.

● **Hydatidiform mole,** an abnormality in pregnancy, means that the embryo does not develop, only the placenta, which produces a large amount of human chorionic gonadatrophin (HCG), the pregnancy hormone which is checked when you have a pregnancy test. You will probably miscarry, or the placenta will need to be removed using dilation and curettage (D and C). You'll need to be carefully monitored to see that your HCG levels come down again, which will generally happen in a matter of weeks. In a small number of cases the levels stay high, suggesting a form of cancer of the uterus (which usually responds well to treatment). If you have had a hydatidiform mole you should not take the pill until your test result shows you are completely free of HCG.

● **Severe depression** could be the result of some kind of hormonal disturbance. Even if it is not, the pill itself might make it worse (this happens less with the lower dose pills currently available than it did with previous high dose ones). It's probably best to wait until you get over the depression before taking the pill.

Many of the factors in this list will vary in degree from woman to woman, and they are not all what in medical terminology are called 'absolute contra-indications' – i.e. definite reasons why you shouldn't take the pill. This is one of the reasons why it is so important to discuss your medical history in detail with your doctor before having it prescribed. There are other rare conditions, such as Crohn's disease and chorea, which are also likely to be contra-indications. But if you have had, say, one episode of slightly raised blood pressure, this may not be a reason in itself not to have the pill.

How to take the pill

Most combination pills come in a pack of 21 or 22, each section marked with a day of the week. These are taken every day until the pack is finished, followed by seven (or six, with the 22-pill pack) pill-free days during which you will have a withdrawal bleed.

You should always start triphasic or biphasic pills on the first day of your period. It is vital that you take them in the right order, so you get the right sequence of pills.

You can also get 'everyday' (ED) packs, which contain seven dummy pills which are taken after the 21 hormone-containing ones. You can get these if you think you might forget to stop and start the pill every month. It's important to take these packs in the right order otherwise you may not be protected from pregnancy. You will have a withdrawal bleed when you take the pills from the red section of the pack – these are the dummy pills.

You can start taking the combination pill on the first day of your period. This means that the pill will start working immediately, and you can rely on it as a contraceptive from then on. If you take it on day five of your period you should use another contraceptive as well (like a condom or diaphragm with spermicide) for the first seven of pill-taking. You will need to do this if you are taking the everyday pill too, as the first pills you take are dummy ones. If you are in doubt, look at the manufacturer's instructions that come with the packet, and ask your doctor or clinic for an information leaflet on how to take your pill.

The regular routine that follows of 21 days on, seven days off, is then straightforward, *as long as you remember to take your pill*. Try to choose a time of day at which you can incorporate it into your routine. Most women choose to take it last thing at night, or when they get up in the morning. It is best to take it about the same time every day, to within an hour or so, so that you have a consistent and even dose from day to day.

What to do if you forget a pill

It is highly likely that some day, some time, you'll forget to take a pill. This could mean that the contraceptive's reliability effect is reduced, and you could ovulate. But this will depend on how late you remember that you haven't taken it, so don't assume you are immediately unprotected from pregnancy.

If you take it *up to 12 hours late* then the contraceptive effect won't be decreased. So if you forgot to take it last thing at night, take it in the morning, then take the next pill at the usual time later that same day.

If more than 12 hours have elapsed since you should have taken the pill (you only remember to take it in the middle of the next afternoon, for instance), take the missed pill immediately, and the next one at the usual time that evening. But being without the pill for this length of time could mean you are unprotected and could ovulate. So keep taking the pill in the normal way, but use an additional contraceptive – either the condom, or diaphragm or spermicide) for the next 14 days.

If you miss *more than one pill* (making you 24 or more hours late), take *one* as soon as you remember, and another at your regular time that day. If you are on a tri- or biphasic pill take the last of the pills you should have taken. From then on take a daily pill as usual. Don't take the rest of the missed pills – you might as well throw those pills away to avoid confusion about which you should take and which you shouldn't. You will also need to use another contraceptive for 7 days, or stop having sex with penetration during that time. Sometimes if you forget a few pills, you might have a small withdrawal bleed before you are due for one. Keep taking the pills as usual if this happens. Until recently women were advised to use additional contraception for 14 days. This has now been found to be an over- cautious guideline. The contraceptive effect of the pill is in fact restored after only a week of taking it.

If you miss a pill at the end of the packet you will find that the seven days of extra precautions extends into the pill-free week. If this is the case you should start the next packet immediately with no break for a withdrawal bleed, as well as using an extra contraceptive or avoiding penetration for the next seven days. If you are on an ED (Every Day) pill you should skip the week of dummy pills and go straight to the first of the active contraceptive pills. You need to do this because otherwise you would be extending the pill-free time so that there would be an even greater chance of ovulation. Ovulation is less likely if you miss a pill in the middle of the packet. But the possibility of pregnancy is always there whenever you forget a pill, so it makes sense to follow the guidelines on additional contraception if you do forget one.

If you stick to the routine described, it is very unlikely that you could get pregnant. Even if you don't have the usual withdrawal bleed during the pill-free days at the end of the packet, you should not assume you are pregnant until you have had a positive pregnancy test result. Stop taking the pill if you don't have a withdrawal bleed after missing pills, but carry on using a barrier method until you have a test. Many women have got pregnant because they assumed they were *already* pregnant, and stopped using contraception altogether.

If you have had intercourse while you weren't taking the pill and think there is a chance of pregnancy, you can have *post-coital contraception* (see page 140) within 72 hours of the unprotected sex.

Upset stomach

Sickness or diarrhoea could mean that you don't absorb the pill properly, so the effect is similar to forgetting a pill. The pill could, if you vomit, come straight back up. If you have diarrhoea the pill could go straight through you.

It takes about three hours for the pill to enter your bloodstream once you've taken it. If you are sick after this time you can assume the pill has been properly absorbed. But if you vomit *within three hours* it's as if you haven't taken a pill at all. In this case you should take another pill immediately. If you do this within 12 hours of taking the first pill, and you are not sick again, you should take the next pill at the usual time and go on as usual for the rest of the packet. But if you go on being sick at frequent intervals, so the pill never gets a chance to be absorbed, you should behave the same way as you would if you'd missed a pill (or pills) for more than 12 hours – this means using a barrier method for the next 7 days, or no intercourse.

If you have diarrhoea *within 12 hours* of taking the pill, it may not have been absorbed, so the routine is the same as if you'd forgotten one – a barrier method for the next 7 days, or no intercourse.

Drugs that reduce the contraceptive effect of the pill

There are a number of drugs that interact with the pill in such a way that the contraceptive effect is lessened. For this reason you should always check with your doctor if you are prescribed another drug, for either long- or short-term use. Some *anti-convulsants* (used to treat epilepsy) can have this effect, as can some *antibiotics* and *tranquillisers*.

If you have epilepsy and are on a regular prescription of anti-convulsants it is likely that you will have discussed this with your doctor. If the drug you take is a phenobarbitone (brand name Luminal) or a barbiturate (brand names Tegretol, Zarontin, Mysoline or Epanutin) absorption of the pill can be reduced by enzymes produced by the liver in response to the anti-convulsants' stimulative effect. This can be countered by taking a higher oestrogen (50mg) pill.

Antibiotics known to effect the pill include 'broad spectrum' drugs such as ampicillin and tetracycline, and rifampicin, used to treat tuberculosis. If you are on a short course of antibiotics, perhaps for the treatment of a one-off infection, you may have to use an additional contraceptive while you are taking the antibiotics and for 14 days afterwards. It appears that the long-term use of a low dose tetracycline (normally prescribed for acne) doesn't affect the pill.

THE PILL AND YOUR HEALTH   119

You should not take the pill if you are on chloral hydrate, dichloralphenazone, or glutethimide – all *hypnotics*. If you are on short-term treatment from a tranquilliser like Largactil or Equanil you could either use a higher dose pill, or an additional contraceptive for the days while you take the tranquilliser and 14 days afterwards.

If you are on any drug as well as the pill and breakthrough bleeding occurs it could mean a drug interaction and that the contraceptive effect has been lessened – consult your doctor if this happens.

A few drugs actually increase the effect of the pill. Large daily doses of vitamin C (0.5-1mg) enhance the effect of the oestrogen as if you were taking a higher dose pill, with an accompanying increase in the risk of circulatory disease. Septrin (an antibiotic often used for treating cystitis) and Flagyl (used to treat vaginal infections like gardenerella and trichomonas) also increase the effect of the pill.

The effect of some other drugs can be interfered with when you are on the pill, or the likelihood of bad effects can be increased. These include drugs used to treat diabetes, migraine, depression and tension.

Always tell your doctor that you are on the pill before being prescribed any other drug.

The pill and your health – physical effects
The pill is a *systemic* drug – its influence is not confined only to the process of reproduction, but to your whole body. Just as the naturally occurring hormones in the menstrual cycle produce generalised physiological changes, so do the synthetic hormones in the pill. As a result the likelihood of some serious physical problems are increased, and some decreased. These additional changes are usually described as *side effects*, but that's a term which is to some extent misleading. They are *other effects* of the pill, apart from the major and intended effect of stopping pregnancy, and are the result of the generalised influence of the pill. Such changes are only to be

expected with a systemic drug of this kind, and they are not a subsidiary or surprising event, as the term 'side effects' implies.

The effects of the pill on the cardiovascular system were the first noted, best charted and conclusively researched. It is clear that the oestrogen in the combined pill is responsible for these, a finding that has led to the introduction of low oestrogen pills and to better screening for physical problems that could increase the risk of pill-related cardiovascular disease. High doses of progestogen may also play some part in the development of cardiovascular and other problems, and in the phased pill the progestogen level has now been reduced by 30 per cent.

Dispute about the increase of the risk of cancer (particularly of the breast and the cervix) continues, and those who think this risk is increased relate it to progestogen in the pill. Many other effects – of oestrogen, progestogen, and the combination of the two – are clear and proven, but research on still more continues.

Cardiovascular disease

Increased risk of disease of the cardiovascular system – the heart, veins and arteries, and blood – is definitely associated with the pill. Very few women actually end up suffering such a disease as a result of taking the pill, but of those that do *thrombosis* is the most common. A thrombosis is a blood clot that forms in a vein or artery, which could lead to severe pain, a stroke, a heart attack or, in very rare cases, death.

The oestrogen in the pill makes thrombosis more likely because it increases the amount of the blood *platelets* that make blood clot. These substances stop us haemorrhaging as a result of a cut or graze, and are what is missing in those who suffer from haemophilia. If you are a young, healthy and active non-smoking woman this pill-risk is very low indeed, because your body produces other blood chemicals which counteract the clotting effect. This protective response is reduced if you are over 40, are very overweight, or if you smoke.

For this reason very few women over 45 take the combined pill – if they are on the pill at all it is likely to be the progestogen-only pill (see page 133), which doesn't carry these risks. Most of the women who develop circulatory disease on the pill are smokers. Even if you are a smoker and *don't* take the pill, the risk of this disease is increased. Women who don't take the pill but who smoke are up to four times more likely to have a heart attack, for instance.

But the addition of the oestrogen in the pill multiplies the risk. And for smokers, the age factor is especially important. One study found that smokers of 41-50 who took the pill ran a risk of heart attack between 350 to 800 times greater than non-smoking women of the same age who were also on the pill. It seems clear that it's the smoking that is responsible for this risk, and you can greatly reduce it if you give up smoking. If you can't manage to give up, you should think about using another form of contraception once you are over 35.

Smoking while taking the pill also appears to increase the risk of certain types of stroke, but age seems to be the major factor. One kind of stroke (subarachnoid haemorrhage) is frequently preceded by high blood pressure (see below) which is one of the reasons why your blood pressure needs to be monitored while you're taking the pill. If your blood pressure is normal, the risk of this stroke is very small. High blood pressure can be a sign of other cardiovascular problems too, which may or may not be related to the pill. If they are, your blood pressure should come down once you stop taking it.

There are a number of other factors which could make cardiovascular disease more likely, and which should have been discussed with your doctor before you were prescribed the pill (see page 113). If none of them applies to you, and you are fit, young and don't smoke, the pill poses a very small risk. But you should still know the signs of thrombosis, stroke or heart attack, and see a doctor immediately if any of these happen to you:

- fainting or collapse
- severe pain in the chest or stomach
- painful and swollen calf
- abnormal and severe headache
- disturbance of speech or vision
- numbness, tingling or weakness in an arm or leg
- breathlessness and/or coughing up blood

Cancer
Research on cancer and the pill produces both good and bad news. It

appears that taking the pill actually reduces the risk of cancers of the ovary and the endometrium (uterine lining). Taking the pill for one year reduces the risk of endometrial cancer by half. The risk is not further reduced if you take the pill for longer than this. It is worth noting that pregnancy has a similar effect. The risk of ovarian cancer appears to be reduced by around 40 per cent if you take the pill, and remains lower for up to ten years after you stop taking the pill.

Changes in lifestyle and reproductive patterns in the years since the pill was introduced have been thought to be responsible for the rise in the incidence of both breast and cervical cancer, particularly in younger women. Two studies in 1983, however, linked the development of both of these types of cancer with pill-taking, isolating the progestogen in the pill as the cause.

The risk of development of breast cancer was described in one study as being increased mainly in women who had taken the pill for at least five years under the age of 25. Another study linked an increased risk of cervical cancer to long-term pill use (six to eight years).

It is very difficult to draw clear conclusions from either of these studies, or the critical outcry from the medical profession and family planning agencies that followed. One of the major criticisms was that progestogen potency (see page 111) wasn't taken into account in one of the studies. An American research project on cancer and steroid hormones (the CASH study) has shown no link between the pill and breast cancer. It may be many years before definitive evidence is available on this, mainly because breast cancer tends to be a disease of older women, so any marked change in breast cancer rates may not show up until the pill-taking generation is in its 60s and 70s.

Subsequent research on cervical cancer has confirmed that women who take the pill are more likely to develop the abnormal cell condition that precedes it (neoplasia), but the reason for this is not fully known. Sex with more than one partner, increasing the likelihood of the cancer-implicated papilloma virus, has been put forward as the cause of the increasing incidence of this disease (and as the reason why women who use barrier methods are less likely to get it). But even if this is the case, it may be that taking the pill *accelerates* the development of invasive cervical cancer in women who already have abnormal cervical cells.

But researchers are a long way from definitive results on both these cancers and the pill, so that you have to weigh up a whole lot of unknown factors when you make the decision to use the pill, or to continue taking it. Doctors give conflicting advice about what to do if you are on the pill and have an abnormal cervical smear – should you stay on the pill or not? At the very least women who take the pill should have regular cervical smears, but even this need is not properly met because the government won't provide the money needed for an efficient and comprehensive cervical screening service in every health district. The NHS will not pay GPs for smears done on women who are under 35, or if they are done more often than once every five years. Some cancer specialists have proposed that women in what may turn out to be the high-risk group for cervical cancer (those who have taken the pill for five years or more under the age of 25 and have had a number of sexual partners) should have a cervical smear every year, others say every two or three years.

What *is* clear is that if a cervical smear does show pre-cancerous cells, a simple surgical treatment is then possible which will stop cancer itself developing. Screening is therefore vital, so you should do your best to get a regular smear (at least every three to five years) if you think you are at risk of cervical cancer. Until there is more evidence of what effect the pill has on abnormal cells and the later development of cancer, it makes sense to stop taking it if you have an abnormal smear result – but many doctors will disagree with this suggestion.

It has been confirmed that women who are on the pill for eight years or more have an increased likelihood of getting liver cancer. The risk of getting it is twenty times more likely, but since the risk is already very low this means that the number of women who will actually get it is quite small. It has been estimated that the pill will be responsible for up to 12 deaths from liver cancer per year in England and Wales of women under 50. It is not known whether some pills are more likely than others to cause liver cancer.

The pill has also been implicated in the development of malignant melanoma (a kind of skin cancer) in young women who have taken it for two years or more, but there is no definite evidence of this, and research results conflict.

All these known and suspected links with cancer make decisions very difficult for any woman who is considering the pill. For some, the research of 1983 was enough to make them go off the pill. Others decided that the known benefits outweighed the unknown risks. All of those who take or have taken the pill have to live with the fact that it may take many years before the genuine risks are known, and present suspicions confirmed or not.

Pelvic inflammatory disease, vaginal and urinary infections

Your risk of developing pelvic inflammatory disease (PID) is considerably reduced when you are on the pill; it is 50 per cent lower than if you weren't using any contraception at all, and even smaller than if you were using a barrier method (see page 162). This effect is likely to continue only for as long as you are on the pill, as it's probably due to the pill-induced thickening of the cervical mucus which may prevent infection entering the uterus.

There have also been reports that trichomonas infection (which produces an irritating foamy discharge) is less likely if you take the pill. The risk of toxic shock syndrome (TSS) may also be reduced, maybe because the withdrawal bleed you have on the pill is so much lighter than a menstrual period.

It is possible that the pill, because of the hormonal changes which affect your vagina, could make it more likely that you get thrush. You can be treated for this without the pill's effectiveness being diminished.

There is one infection against which the pill appears to offer no defence – chlamydia. You can have this condition without realising you've got it, until it results in pelvic inflammatory disease. This could mean infected and scarred fallopian tubes, which make it impossible for you to get pregnant. An American research paper has suggested that the risk of chlamydia is three times as great if you take the pill. The rate of other diseases which lead to PID, such as gonorrhea, was down in pill-users, but there was a considerable rise in incidence of chlamydia. The study was criticised because it didn't take into account the number of sexual partners the subjects had had, and it is impossible at this point to draw clear conclusions: does the pill actually make you more vulnerable to chlamydia, or simply provide no defence?

Only for the past few years has chlamydia been recognised as a major sexually transmitted disease (STD). In America it is now the most common STD. In this country it is estimated that chalmydia infection makes up 50 per cent of those conditions diagnosed as non-specific urethritis, but it is rarely tested for. And because, in almost three quarters of the women who have it, it is present without symptoms, it is likely to be much more widespread than is recognised. Chlamydia infection is likely to be more apparent in men, with urethritis as the main symptom. So if your sexual partner develops this, make sure you get tested for a range of STDs *including* chlamydia. It is also worth having a general check for STDs whenever you start a new sexual relationship. If you have more than one sexual partner at a time, or if your partner has more than one, you should also have regular check-ups.

Ovarian cysts

The pill provides protection against the kind of ovarian cyst that can develop when you are having a natural menstrual cycle. This kind of cyst is related directly to ovulation, so if you are not ovulating (which you don't on the pill) there will be little risk of this.

Withdrawal and breakthrough bleeds

Menstrual problems you may have had before going on the pill (pre-menstrual syndrome, heavy or painful periods, etc.) are not likely to occur with such frequency when you are no longer having a menstrual cycle. You don't have the cyclical hormonal changes which can produce pre-menstrual symptoms like swollen and painful breasts or depression (though taking a phased pill may mean you still have some of these symptoms). Because you are no longer ovulating you will not have *Mittelschmerz*, the ovulation pain some women get in the middle of the menstrual cycle.

The withdrawal bleed itself is likely to be lighter and less painful than a menstrual period. This is because the lining of the uterus shed during the pill-free week is much thinner than the lining shed during a menstrual period. The withdrawal bleed is likely to be very regular – most women on the pill know to within a few hours when the withdrawal bleed is due.

You can defer a withdrawal bleed if you don't want it to coincide with some particular event – if you are travelling, or sitting exams. You can take two packs one after the other without a break (if you want to avoid the bleed altogether one month), or extend the number of days you take the pill by taking some out of the next packet (stopping them a few days later and having the withdrawal bleed after that). Once you have had the seven-day break from the pill you should start a new packet as usual.

It is more difficult to do this if you are on a phased pill. You can put off the withdrawal bleed for *up to ten days* by daily taking the third-phase pills from a new packet, and then having the break and withdrawal bleed after that. If you want to avoid a withdrawal bleed altogether, you will have to switch to a higher hormone-level brand for the next three weeks, returning to your original brand immediately afterwards. This means you take three packs in succession without a break or withdrawal bleed *for nine weeks*. You'll have to discuss this with your doctor who is able to prescribe the different brand.

Usually, for the sake of keeping the total amount of pill hormones you ingest as low as possible, stick to the usual routine of three weeks on and one week off the pill. And remember you can only *postpone* a period – if you stop taking the pills early so as to bring forward the time of the withdrawal bleed, you will be in the same position as you would be if you had missed pills by mistake – with a chance that you could ovulate and get pregnant if you had intercourse without using an additional contraceptive.

Breakthrough bleeding, perhaps in the middle of a pill packet, could be due to not having enough hormone in the pill you are currently taking to maintain the lining of the uterus. You may need to switch to a higher dose pill in order to stop the breakthrough bleeds. You can also have a breakthrough bleed if you have forgotten a pill (or pills), or if a drug you are taking is interfering with the pill's effect (see pages 116 and 118), and this could be an indication that the pill's reliability as a contraceptive is being interfered with too.

Protection from endometriosis

The endometrium is the lining of the uterus which in a menstrual cycle bleeds during a period. *Endometriosis* means that this same material is present elsewhere in the reproductive organs as well as in the uterus, and it responds to the hormonal changes of the menstrual cycle in the same way, resulting in bleeding and pain during menstrual periods, and possibly bleeding in the middle of the menstrual cycle too. The causes of this condition vary, and it can be treated with antibiotics. Some brands of pill may also help, because the pill stops the menstrual cycle which makes the condition more painful.

Breast changes

Many women find their breasts get bigger when they are taking the pill, mainly when it is first taken. Your breasts may also feel uncomfortable and a bit bloated at first. This may be annoying, but does not mean there is anything wrong with your breasts. The phased pills can make your breasts feel swollen during the last phase of the pack, and this may happen every month.

The pill stops the cyclical hormonal changes that normally affect your breasts, which can make them lumpy and over-sensitive in the days before a period. This and other breast disorders which produce non-cancerous lumps are called *benign breast disease*, and are far less likely if you take the pill.

The combined pill should be avoided if you are breast-feeding, because it depresses milk production. This will not happen if you take the progestogen-only pill (see page 133), but a small amount of the progestogen hormone will be transmitted to the baby. At present there is no evidence of any harmful effect on the child, but follow-up research continues into the health of children who have ingested progestogen in breast milk. Children monitored up to the age of 20 have not shown any ill effects.

Headaches and migraine

It is difficult to know whether an increased frequency of headaches has coincided with or been caused by the pill. You'll need to check out whether there might be a reason other than the pill if you start getting headaches more often – you might need to wear glasses, or deal with some source of tension in your life. If the headaches have a regular and apparently cyclical pattern, maybe during every pill-free week, you may be able to solve this by changing to a pill with a different strength of progestogen or to a phased pill.

Migraine headaches might also be more likely during the week you are not taking the pill. If you already suffer from migraine the pill could make attacks more frequent, less frequent, or not alter the pattern at all. If they are made more frequent this may improve by changing to a lower dose brand of pill, but you may have to give up the pill altogether.

Any unusual and sharp headache or disturbed vision or speech means you should see your doctor immediately – it could be a sign of cardiovascular problems.

Allergies and viral infections

Not much is known about the effect of the pill in relation to allergies and vulnerability to viral infection. It is known that it is possible (in rare cases) to be allergic to the synthetic hormones in the pill itself, but it is not clear what effect the pill has on other allergies. Eczema, hay fever and asthma (all of which can be brought on by an allergic reaction) are more common in women who are on the pill. The likelihood of some other skin diseases may also be increased (see below).

It has also been found that you are more likely to get virus infections (which could be anything from influenza or cystitis) when you are on the pill. All of these findings point to the possibility that the pill in some way affects the body's immune system (which protects against allergy and viruses).

Skin changes

The pill (especially the higher dose brands) depletes the amount of oil the skin produces, so problems related to this (greasy hair, spots, excessive earwax) may well be dealt with by the pill, especially if it is one higher in oestrogen.

The amount of hair on your face and body may also reduce when you go on the pill, but if you already are quite hairy you could find the reverse happens – you may have more hair when you are on the pill. This may also be helped by a change of pill. If it doesn't, the amount of hair should return to normal once you are off the pill.

Chloasma is a kind of brown mark, which looks a bit like a stain, which can appear on the face of white women on the pill. It can also happen when you are pregnant (when it is called *pregnancy mask*). It appears when your face is exposed to a lot of sunlight, and may never fade entirely, even after you've stopped taking the pill. You may also find your skin's tolerance of bright sunlight is reduced, so that you come out in hives (itchy and sore patches) when you've been in the sun. This is a rare condition but more common in pill-users, and it doesn't always stop once you are off the pill.

Eye changes

The pill sometimes affects the amount of fluid on the surface of the eye. This can affect a few women who wear contact lenses. The problem can be helped by having your lenses changed, or by taking a lower dose pill.

Nausea and other intestinal problems

Nausea used to be much more of a problem with earlier higher dose pills, but may still happen when you first start taking the pill, and continue to happen each time you start the packet after the seven-day break. It is likely to clear up altogether once you've been on the pill for three months or so. If it doesn't, you could try a lower dose brand.

In past studies the pill has been implicated in the development of gall stones and gall bladder disease, and progestogen has been thought responsible. It is now thought that the pill does not actually cause this, but may increase the risk of it if you already have a tendency to gall bladder problems.

Jaundice, similar to the jaundice that can happen in pregnancy, is a liver disease which can also be caused by the pill, or brought on again if you have had it before. This is why you shouldn't take the pill if you have had jaundice or any other liver disease in the past (see page 113).

Duodenal ulcers may be less likely if you take the pill, but the reason for this is not known. Gum disease may be more likely (as it is when you are pregnant), so regular dental checks are important.

Rheumatoid arthritis and muscular problems

There has been evidence that the pill provides protection against the development of rheumatoid arthritis (a disorder of the joints, rare in women of pill-taking age), but this has recently been disputed by an American study. There has been evidence that *carpal tunnel syndrome*, a painful swelling around the nerves in the wrist, is more likely in pill users. This condition is very rare in pre-menopausal women, usually occurring only during pregnancy in women of this age group.

Weight gain

Low dose pills are much less likely to produce weight gain than earlier brands, because of the lower hormone levels. If they do, weight gain is most likely to happen in the first few months of taking the pill. It may be caused by water retention (more frequent with progestogen-dominant pills) or by an increase of body fat because your appetite is bigger.

If you are experiencing water retention you will probably find that you lose a few pounds during the pill-free week. You will lose the weight when you go off the pill. If weight gain is caused by increased appetite you can either restrict the amount of food you eat, or (preferably) increase your energy output by becoming more physically active.

Psychological effects – depression and loss of interest in sex

Those who promote the pill are keen to emphasise its positive psychological effects. Free from worry about unplanned pregnancy, they suggest, women feel generally happier and enjoy sex more. But it is clear that some women do find they get more depressed on the pill, and that there is an accompanying loss of libido (interest in sex). Some women, who don't feel depressed, also experience a drop in their level of sexual desire. This may be accompanied by a decrease in vaginal lubrication during arousal, and even a decrease in the sensitivity of the vulva and intensity of orgasm.

It may be impossible to know exactly whether your particular depression or decrease in sexual desire is a result of taking the pill. It may be caused by more than one reason – tiredness, relationship difficulties or other health problems.

Though some women find that depression lifts and desire returns soon after stopping the pill, this may not be the only thing worth trying. It is known that the pill can reduce the absorption of vitamin B6 (also called pyridoxine), which is known to be a chemical with important psychological effects. So taking a vitamin B6 supplement, and eating more B6-rich foods (such as wholegrains, yeast and fish) may help if this is the cause of the problem.

A lower dose pill, or change of brand, may also help. If none of these suggestions works for you, it may be worth going off the pill so you can get a better idea of whether it is the cause of the problem.

You should have regular check-ups when you are on the pill, at which your weight and blood pressure are taken. You'll probably have one check-up after three months on it, and then have them every six months thereafter. But return to your doctor if you are worried by anything that you think may be caused by the pill.

If you get pregnant while you're on the pill

If you take the pill exactly as prescribed, and its reliability is not interfered with in any way (by sickness, diarrhoea or drug interaction), it is almost certain that you won't get pregnant. But if the contraceptive action is depleted in some way, and you do get pregnant, you may not be aware of the pregnancy for some weeks, and continue to take the pill. It should be clear that you may be pregnant by the time you reach the pill-free week, as you almost certainly won't have a withdrawal bleed. But sometimes you can have a very light withdrawal bleed even if you are pregnant and, believing the pill is still working and you are not pregnant, you may go on taking it.

There has been a considerable amount of research into what effect taking the pill has on a developing foetus. There is no indication that the rate of miscarriage or infant mortality is increased, and most research does not show any link between taking the pill during pregnancy, and birth defects in the baby. But one American study did find this link in women who were taking the pill in early pregnancy, and in the cycle immediately before conception. And some British research found a link between *neural tube defects* (the best known of which is spina bifida) and pill-taking – both during pregnancy and in the three months before conception. But no other research has confirmed this finding.

It is impossible to know whether there are any really long-term effects of hormones on the foetus. Although the pill has been used and researched for thirty years it is impossible to know whether anything happens to the baby when it is over thirty. So although most of the current research is reassuring, and many women have taken the pill with no apparent ill effects on their babies, it may be many years until there is conclusive evidence one way or the other.

After the pill – the return of the menstrual cycle – getting pregnant

It may take three months or so before your usual menstrual cycle returns. In a minority of women it may take longer than this to have a period. *Post-pill amenorrhea* is thought to be related to the kind of cycle you had before you went on the pill. If your periods were irregular or infrequent before taking the pill they are likely to be so afterwards too. But for some women the pill seems to bring out the tendency for irregular periods, and you may have to wait for several months before you have a period. But whatever the reason for your lack of periods, you should see your doctor if you still haven't had one after six months.

Once you have been off the pill for three months (assuming your periods have started again) your chances of conceiving a first pregnancy may depend on how old you are. Recent British research has found that older women who come off the pill do seem to be affected by it, so that conception is delayed. Of those who had been using the pill, 17.5 per cent had still not had a child two years after they had stopped the pill, as against 11.5 per cent of those using other methods of contraception. Three years after stopping the pill, these figures reduced to 12.7 per cent and 10 per cent respectively. This effect may be related to long-term use of the pill (which may well apply to older women), as well as to an interaction between the effects of the pill and of ageing itself. There is no evidence at this point that taking the pill has a permanent effect on fertility. Further research continues.

There is no evidence for an increased risk of miscarriage, infant mortality or birth defects if you get pregnant after taking the pill. But the possible delay in the return of fertility may mean that you want to go off the pill a few months before you think you will want to conceive. This gives your body a chance to establish a regular menstrual cycle.

There is, even if you haven't used the pill, a one-in-ten chance that you won't be able to get pregnant anyway. This may be related to a problem either in you or your sexual partner (something you could only discover by having fertility tests). Most doctors won't think it worth investigating until you've been trying to get pregnant for at least a year. It can be enormously depressing to think of all that time you've spent using contraception when there may have been no need for it. You may also feel (or know, if you've been pregnant before) that there might have been a chance you were fertile in earlier years, and you missed your opportunity to have a baby. It's easy to feel cheated by the medical profession and family planners if this happens to you – the emphasis of all the information you may have got was on *stopping* pregnancy, and it sounded as if you would always be able to have a baby whenever you wanted to – all you had to do was to stop contraception. Even though this is true in the majority of women it can be very hard to bear if it turns out not to apply to you.

The progestogen-only pill

Also known as the POP or mini-pill, the progestogen-only pill does not contain any oestrogen as the combined pill does, hence its name.

It is slightly less reliable than the combination pill (around 98 per cent) and there is an increased margin of error if you forget to take it. It is mainly prescribed for women who can't take the oestrogen in the combined pill, and who run an increased risk of the oestrogen-related disorders described in the preceding section – principally cardiovascular problems. It is very effective for women over 40.

How the progestogen-only pill works

It is not exactly clear how this pill works, but it seems there are a number of effects on the reproductive system which, put together, stop conception. It does not usually inhibit ovulation, but instead inhibits fertilisation. The progestogen-only pill's main effect is to thicken the cervical mucus that lies at the entrance to the uterus, so that sperm cannot penetrate and gain access to the egg. The lining of the uterus is also changed, so that any fertilised egg cannot implant itself. It also seems that the fallopian tubes are affected so that they do not move the egg from the ovary to the uterus as they do during the menstrual cycle.

Progestogen-only pills currently available

Brand name	Description	Type of progestogen	Amount in mg
Femulen	28 white pills	Ethynodiol diacetate	0.5
Neogest	35 brown pills	Norgestrel	0.075
Noriday	3x28 yellow pills	Norethisterone	0.35
Norgeston	35 white pills	Levonorgestrel	0.03
Micronor	3x38 white pills	Norethisterone	0.35
Microval	35 white pills	Levonorgestrel	0.03

Who can take the progestogen-only pill?

There is no evidence that the POP poses risks of cardiovascular disease, as it is thought to be the oestrogen in the combined pill which is responsible for this. So if you have some of the health problems or medical history which increase this risk, and you can't take the combined pill (see page 112), the POP may be an alternative. Most doctors will probably not prescribe it if you have had cardiovascular disease itself, but could well do so if you haven't but are in a higher risk group – you are over 45, or have had episodes of raised blood pressure in the past, for example. But in general the *contra-indications* (reasons why it shouldn't be taken) are the same as for the combined pill, so check for these on page 113. However, there are other aspects of your medical history which could also mean that you should not take it:

● **Irregular periods for which the cause is not known.** Because the POP may make your cycle even more irregular, it will make diagnosis and treatment of this more difficult.

● **Breast cancer.** Because this is a hormonally-based cancer, the POP might cause problems.

● **Previous ectopic pregnancy.** The POP increases the risk of an ectopic pregnancy (one outside the uterus, usually in a fallopian tube), so if you have had this before the risk will be considerably increased.

● **Abnormal cervical cells.** As cancer of the cervix is a hormonal cancer, it may be better not to take any sort of hormonal contraception (see page 121).

● **Hydatidiform mole.** If you have had this rare abnormality of pregnancy (see page 114) you should wait until your human chorionic gonadatrophin (pregnancy hormone) level is down before taking the POP.

● **Drug interaction.** This is more or less the same as for the combined pill, with the exception of antibiotics, which don't appear to affect the POP's reliability.

How to take the progestogen-only pill

The POP is taken every day, without the break you have with the combination pill. Different brands are presented in different numbers of pills per packet (see above) but this doesn't make any difference to the pill's effect, since each one is the same and is taken every day.

When you start taking the POP you should take the first pill on the first day of your period. You should not rely on it as a contraceptive for 14 days – you can either use a barrier method, or not have intercourse.

If you are switching from the combined pill, take the POP on the day after the last combination pill. You can rely on it immediately, just as you can rely on it if you start taking it on the day of an abortion or miscarriage. If you have just had a baby, you can start taking the pill from seven days after the birth (see page 139). It will be reliable immediately.

The effect of the pill is at its strongest (and therefore it is at its most reliable as a contraceptive) about four hours after it is taken. You should therefore set the time you take it as four hours before you usually have sex. Women are often advised to take it at around 7 p.m. – fine if you have intercourse at about the same time every evening, but inappropriate if you usually have intercourse in the afternoon. So when you first take it, choose what *you* think is the best time to take the pill. From then on you should stick to this time, day in day out, because the pill's reliability will be affected if you take it three or more hours late. This regularity is thought to be more important for the pill's reliability than the choice of time you take it. Once you've been taking the pill for a few weeks you can rely on it as a contraceptive at any time of day.

What to do if you forget a progestogen-only pill

Because the POP is less powerful than the combined pill, the contraceptive effect can be diminished if you take it *more than three hours late*. If you are late taking just one pill, take it as soon as you remember, and take the next pill at the usual time. But though it is clear there will be some loss of the pill's reliability, it is not clear how long this will last if you take the pill regularly from then on – the current advice is to use additional contraception for 48 hours after the late pill. (This is a revision of the guidelines which suggested you would be unprotected for 14 days if you took the pill late.)

If you forget more than one pill, you should take the next pill at the usual time, and continue to do so from then on. Reliability could well be affected, so use an extra contraceptive for the next 48 hours. If you've had intercourse without additional contraception during the time you've forgotten the pills, there's a chance you could already be pregnant. Given the possibility of an adverse effect of the POP on the developing foetus (see page 139) you may decide it is best to stop taking the pill, and to use another contraceptive until you know for sure whether or not you are pregnant. If you then have a period, or negative pregnancy test, you can start taking the pill again as usual, but you should wait 48 hours until relying on it, since you are starting from scratch again.

A similar routine applies if you are sick or have diarrhoea when on the POP, because this can prevent the pill from being absorbed. If you vomit *within three hours* of taking the pill you should take another pill as soon as you can. If you bring this one up as well it's as if you have missed a pill. Return to regular pill-taking as soon as you can, but use an additional contraceptive for the next 48 hours. If you have missed more than one pill, and didn't use additional contraception during the time you'd forgotten, you may want to stop taking the pill because of the chance you are already pregnant (see above). If you have diarrhoea *within 12 hours* from the time you took the pill, you should go on taking the pill as usual thereafter, but use extra contraception for the subsequent 48 hours. Again, consider stopping it completely if you think you could have got pregnant during the time you were ill.

The effect of the progestogen-only pill on the menstrual cycle

The POP may or may not stop you ovulating. If it does, you could find you don't have any periods at all while you are on it. Sometimes it may not stop you ovulating every cycle, so that your periods may become irregular. It may also affect the lining of the uterus so that irregular bleeds are frequent. There is very likely to be some change to your menstrual cycle and, in some cases, particularly if there is frequent bleeding, this will be a major disadvantage of the POP. If you had irregular periods before taking the POP you are more likely to have these problems while taking it, but they can happen to women whose cycles have been regular and problem-free in the past. Periods are more likely to be irregular if your body weight is low for your height.

Whilst in some ways you may welcome a complete absence of

periods, it does mean that you can't be entirely sure whether or not you are pregnant (though this is very unlikely if you've been taking the pill in the regular way). You may want to have regular pregnancy tests to check what's actually happening. Irregular bleeding is more likely in the first few months of taking the POP, so you may want to persevere (for up to three months) to see whether it becomes regular again.

If you do have very regular periods on the POP this is likely to be a sign of ovulation, which could mean you are more likely to get pregnant than someone who has an irregular cycle and is therefore ovulating less. Disturbance of the menstrual cycle is the most common reason why women stop taking the POP.

If you are ovulating you could also have some symptoms of pre-menstrual syndrome, though these are likely to be less than if you weren't on the pill at all.

The progestogen-only pill and your health

Because you are taking only the single hormone, health problems are less frequent with the POP than with the combination pill. The menstrual irregularity that this pill can create isn't a health problem as such, even though it may be a clear disadvantage and make you decide to go off it.

The POP does not make thrombosis more likely, as it doesn't increase the clotting factor in the blood as the combined pill does. Blood pressure may be increased a little, but this is much more of a problem with the combined pill.

Unlike the combination pill, which protects against ovarian cysts (see page 125), the risk of these are increased while you are on the POP. You may have some experience of nausea, water retention, loss of libido or fatigue when you first start taking the POP, but this is likely to be much less than on the combination pill and should subside after a few months.

The risk of *ectopic pregnancy* is increased if you use the POP. This could be for a number of reasons. In the rare event of a sperm getting through the thickened cervical mucus and fertilising an egg, the egg is unlikely to be able to implant itself in the uterus because of the changes to the uterus caused by the POP. The fallopian tubes appear not to be able to move the egg down into the uterus so well either, so an egg could be fertilised in a tube and stay there.

Ectopic pregnancy needs immediate treatment, as the tube could rupture and cause considerable internal bleeding. So if you experience either of the following you should see your doctor immediately: severe and continuous pain in one side of your lower abdomen, or pain of this kind after a light or missed period. Diagnosis may be difficult, so make sure you are properly investigated. If it is an ectopic pregnancy you will have to have surgery to have it removed, and risk losing the tube altogether.

Older women, who should not take the combined pill because of the effect of oestrogen, can take the POP. So if you are a non-smoker of 45 or over, or a smoker over 35, you can consider the POP. It still may not be suitable for older smokers, as there may be some increase in the risk of cardiovascular problems in these circumstances.

If you are in your 40s, and your periods stop while you are on the POP, this could be a sign of the menopause. The only way to find out is to go off the pill and use another non-hormonal contraceptive method until you see whether the cycle re-establishes itself. If it does, you can start using the POP again.

The POP does not appear to affect your fertility once you are off it. You can stop taking it at any time, but preferably you should do so on the first day of your period so that you can keep track of your subsequent cycles. If your periods have not returned after six months you should see your doctor.

There is no evidence at the moment that taking the POP immediately before or during early pregnancy results in any birth defects, but until there is long-term research into this it is probably best to avoid doing so if you can (see page 137).

The POP is often offered after childbirth and when you are breast-feeding because it doesn't affect milk production, though there are small changes in levels of fat, protein and lactose. These are not thought to be very great, or to represent any real decrease in the quality of the milk. A small amount of progestogen is known to be transmitted to the baby. There is no evidence as yet that this is harmful, but you still may prefer to use a non-hormonal method instead.

The post-coital pill

The availability of post-coital (after sex) contraception (the morning-after pill) means you can take action to avoid pregnancy *after* you have had sex, if there is a chance that you could have conceived. You could use it if you know that your usual method has failed – a sheath has broken, for instance – or if you haven't used any contraception and you've had sex around the middle of your menstrual cycle.

It has been estimated that there is a 30 per cent chance of getting pregnant each time you have intercourse without contraception in the middle of the cycle, when ovulation is likely. This 'unsafe' time may be a week or more, because sperm can live inside your body for up to five days (see page 87). So even if you didn't have intercourse at the same time as you ovulate, the sex you had a few days before ovulation could result in pregnancy. You can work out your possibly unsafe days by looking at the chapter on fertility awareness.

You can get two kinds of post-coital contraception – the morning-after pill and the IUD. Both should be available from family planning clinics or pregnancy advisory services, and you may be able to get them from your GP. See page 158 for information on the post-coital fitting of the IUD.

What is the morning-after pill?

It has been known for many years that a dose of the synthetic hormones used in the pill can prevent conception *after* intercourse. In the past women were prescribed a five-day course of oestrogen, but now a lower-dose oestrogen and progestogen treatment lasting two days is usually prescribed. This consists of two doses of one or other of two specific contraceptive pills – Eugynon 50 or Ovran. Eugynon 50 is available specially packaged as *PC4* for post-coital use. Only these brands, with their unique balance of two special kinds of oestrogen and progestogen, should be prescribed. They have to be taken *within 72 hours of the time you had unprotected intercourse*. Their effectiveness decreases after this time.

You take two of these pills immediately, and two more 12 hours later. This results in a 99 per cent reliability rate for preventing conception. The pills work by changing the lining of the uterus so that a fertilised egg cannot implant; by stopping ovulation if this has not already happened, or by shortening the menstrual cycle so that you are likely to have a period earlier than usual. How it works to stop conception probably depends on what point in the menstrual cycle it is taken.

Eugynon 50 and Ovran are the only sort that will work. Always get them on prescription from your doctor. Don't borrow ordinary combination pills from a friend.

If you have sex in the days after you've taken the morning-after pill you must still use contraception, or not have intercourse. The pill doesn't stop conception in advance of sex, only *after* sex. You could still ovulate after you've finished the pills.

If you are already on a contraceptive pill

You can use the morning-after pill if you have forgotten one or more of your usual contraceptive pills, and have had sex during that time without additional contraception. You should continue to take your daily pill both during and after the days you are taking the morning-after pill, as well as using a barrier method for the next 14 days, including during the pill-free week if it comes within that time.

Some doctors will not prescribe the morning-after pill if you are already on another contraceptive pill, and will instead advise you to follow the advice on what to do when you miss a pill as described on page 116. If you think it's likely you could have risked pregnancy you can seek alternative help at a family planning clinic, but a pregnancy advisory service may be more likely to prescribe the morning-after pill in these circumstances.

Who can't take the morning-after pill?

Women who run a particular risk of cardiovascular disease or who can't use the ordinary pill (see page 112) for any reason will almost certainly not be able to get the morning-after pill either. If you are in this group the post-coital IUD may be a better alternative. If you are taking any of the drugs which interfere with absorption of the pill (see page 118), you may either have to take a larger amount of the morning-after pill, or discontinue the other drugs for the two days you are taking the morning-after pill. Your doctor should also check your medical history to see whether or not it is okay for you to take these pills.

Nausea

This is one of the major disadvantages of the morning-after pill. More than 60 per cent of women who take it will experience nausea, and 35 per cent will actually vomit. There is less chance of this if you take the pills with food, and the food itself should not be too rich – try to avoid dairy products, greasy or heavily spiced foods, and alcohol.

You will almost certainly be over the nausea by 12 hours after the second dose of the morning-after pills. But if you vomit within three hours of either dose you should return to your doctor. You may need another dose of pills, which this time can be taken with an anti-emetic (anti-sickness) drug. You should also see your doctor again if you have diarrhoea within 12 hours of taking either dose of the pills.

Other effects of the morning-after pill

In the very rare event of the method failing, there may be an increased chance of an ectopic pregnancy. If you have any symptoms of this (see page 164) you must see your doctor immediately.

There is no evidence at present that, if the method fails, the morning-after pill will damage the foetus in any way, but more research on this is needed. You need to consider the implications of this possibility before taking the pills – what would you do if the method failed? Would you want to have an abortion, or to continue the pregnancy? Even though the chance of this method failing is very slight it's important to be as clear as you possibly can about your feelings beforehand.

After the morning-after

Your period may not arrive at its usual time – it could be earlier or later. As long as you have used contraception (or not had intercourse) in the weeks following taking the pill, you will almost certainly not be pregnant. If you suspect there is any chance that you are, you should have a pregnancy test as soon as possible. A blood test or early urine test can diagnose pregnancy within 14 days of conception. A urine test can do this 14 days after the date your period should have started.

You should see the doctor again, either when your next period is due, or within five days of it. Go back to the doctor whether or not you have a period on time.

Contraceptive failure leads to 50 per cent of all requests for morning-after contraception, so it is now very likely that you are reconsidering the method you have been using. You will need to weigh up the advantages and disadvantages of your method once again in the light of what's happened.

If you used post-coital contraception because a condom split, for example, you may now feel you can't rely on them any more. But it's also worth checking once more that your sexual partner knows how to use the condom correctly – he may be leaving no room for the semen when he puts on the condom, making it much more likely to burst when he comes (see page 79). If this is the case there may be no reason to change methods.

If you needed the morning-after pill because your IUD was expelled, you may have to change to another method as it could happen again, but you should check with your doctor – it could be that you would be all right with a different design of IUD. If it was because you forgot to take a pill you may feel less confident that you'll remember to take them in future, though equally it could have the opposite effect.

If you start the pill for the first time after using morning-after contraception, you should wait until the fifth day of your next period to start taking it. This gives you time to make sure that you are having a proper period, and that you are not pregnant.

You may have needed the morning-after pill because you weren't using any form of contraception. No doctor will prescribe these morning-after pills on a regular basis because used like this they will make your cycle irregular. They can't be used more than once in a cycle. If you think there's any chance that you will have intercourse again – this month, next month or whenever – and you don't want to be pregnant, decide now what kind of contraceptive you will use in the future.

Medical attitudes and provision of post-coital contraception

It took some time for post-coital contraception to be widely available, and even now many clinics and GPs don't provide it. And there still exists a punitive attitude towards women who haven't used contraception, who are deemed irresponsible. Or you could find the doctor disbelieves you when you say the condom split, or treats you like an idiot because you forgot your pills.

It's best to try to find a clinic or advisory service which regularly provides post-coital contraception, and where these attitudes are less likely. Otherwise you may have to resign yourself to a lecture from a doctor or family planning nurse. There is no need to agree to using any particular contraceptive in the future if it's a method you don't want to use. Some doctors may be especially keen for you to go on the pill straightaway, but don't if you don't want to.

Injectable contraception

Two long-term injectable contraceptives are available in this country, each made of a different progestogen. Depo Provera, the brand name of the chemical medroxyprogesterone acetate, is the best known and more widely prescribed. Noristerat, which is prescribed less often, is made of a progestogen called norethisterone oenanthate or NET OEN.

Only since 1984 has either of these injections been licensed for long-term use. Before that they were supposed to be prescribed only for short-term use and in certain specific circumstances: following immunisation against rubella (German measles), when conception within three months could result in birth defects, and after a partner's vasectomy, while he is waiting for sperm production to stop. But even before the licence changed, both drugs were given to some women even if these conditions didn't apply.

But now, although the short-term license still applies to Noristerat, Depo Provera can be prescribed just like any other contraceptive, as well as in the circumstances described above. This change in licensing met widespread opposition from many feminist groups, who in the past had campaigned for Depo Provera to be banned.

The reasons for this opposition are complex, and involve both medical and political issues. The major concern is that these injections have been given to Black and working-class women, (who, white middle-class doctors may think, are too unreliable to use any other contraceptive), and that these women don't get proper explanations of what it is and what its other effects on the body might be. Women have reported being given an unnamed 'hormone injection' at the same time as rubella vaccination without any consultation or information about what the extra drug is. So even though there is no evidence that these injectables are any more dangerous to health than other hormonal contraceptives, the fact that they are open to abuse by the medical profession is enough to make many women believe injectable contraception should not be available.

Clearly other contraceptives are also open to the same abuse – a doctor could insert an IUD during an abortion, without telling you this is going to happen. The pill could be prescribed without the doctor informing you of possible bad effects. But it is still within your power to go off these methods if you don't want them – you can stop the pill, or get some other doctor to remove the IUD. Long-term injectable contraception doesn't give you this option. If you have any bad effects you will have to wait until the drug wears off (usually three months) before you're free of them. If you decide you want to get pregnant you will have to wait at least three months and, if you've been on Depo Provera, probably up to a year after the injection before you will be able to conceive. A contraceptive that is more readily reversible (whether hormonal or not) means that you have more control over it while you are taking it.

Possible health risks, particularly the possibility of cancer (see page 148) have also led to opposition to injectables. But such risks are also a very real possibility with other hormonal methods, and not specific to Depo Provera or Noristerat. It could be that the combined pill poses a greater risk of long-term health problems than injectables ... It may be many years before this issue is clear.

Who can't use injectable contraception?

You should not have an injectable contraceptive if the following conditions apply to you:

● **You might be pregnant.**
● **You think you might want to conceive within the next year or two.**
● **You have cancer of the breast or reproductive organs (though some doctors would disagree, and point out that Depo Provera is also used to treat cancer).**
● **If you have just had a baby, miscarriage or abortion.** Injectables given in the first six weeks after these events are more likely to result in irregular and heavy bleeding from the uterus.

You should also check the section on the progestogen-only pill (page 134) to see whether you have any particular problems that mean you shouldn't be on progestogen.

How injectables work and their effects on the body

Both Depo Provera and Noristerat are injected deeply into a muscle, usually a buttock, thigh or arm muscle, and will be active as contraceptives for the next three months. They are usually given within the first five days of your period. If you decide to keep using it, another dose of Depo Provera will be given after every 12 weeks. Noristerat is given every eight weeks.

The contraceptive effect is achieved in a very similar way to the progestogen-only pill (see page 000), with a thickening of cervical mucus and changes in the lining of the uterus. But, unlike the POP, it always stops ovulation.

This absence of ovulation means that you won't have a regular menstrual cycle while you are on an injectable. Your periods will almost certainly become irregular, or they may stop altogether. Lack of periods is very common with injectables, as are frequent and irregular short bleeds. There is no way of telling in advance which might happen to you, but it is said to be more of a problem with Depo Provera than with Noristerat. If the bleeding is very heavy and has gone on for a long time it can be treated with oestrogen, and you may need iron pills if the heavy bleeding has caused anaemia. If oestrogen doesn't work you might have to have dilation and curettage to remove the uterine lining. Irregular bleeding is the main reason why women don't continue with the method.

Once the three months have elapsed it may take some time before you go back to your usual cycle, and your fertility is unlikely to return for a few months. Research has shown that 50 per cent of women who have been on Depo Provera will be menstruating after six months off it. By one year later 85 per cent will be menstruating. There is no evidence of any permanent effect on later fertility. Less is known about how long it will take to menstruate after taking Noristerat, but there are reports that this is likely to happen sooner than with Depo Provera.

It is quite likely that you will gain 1-5kg in weight while you are on the injectable, but you could also gain a lot more than this. Your weight will probably continue to rise the longer you are on it. This may be because the drug increases your appetite, but it's not clear exactly why. Both types of injectable can cause weight gain.

Frequent headaches can also be a problem with injectable contraception, as they can be with other hormonal methods. If this happens with oral contraception you can change brands, and see if a different hormonal balance helps – this is not possible with injectable contraception because of the long-term action. Other unpleasant effects, like a bloated abdomen, will also not subside until the effect of the drug wears off.

Injectable methods appear to provide the same protection against pelvic inflammatory disease as oral contraception does. This is probably because the thickened cervical mucus stops bacteria entering the uterus (see page 124). There has also been a suggestion that injectables reduce the likelihood of thrush.

There may also be an improvement in other conditions. Injectables are thought to reduce hirsutism (a lot of body hair), but some women report the reverse effect. They are also thought to help endometriosis (see page 127). Because of their effect on the blood, sickle cell disease (see page 113) could be improved so that there are fewer attacks of bone pain. Injectables don't increase the clotting factor in the blood as combination pills do, so there is no increased risk of thrombosis.

Breast-feeding

Injectable contraception does not affect the production of breast milk, and in some women may increase or prolong it. The nutritional content is not depleted either. This has been used as an argument in favour of giving it to women in the Third World, though clearly better nutrition and living standards for these women would be a better option.

But, in the same way as happens with the progestogen-only pill, small amounts of the hormone are present in the milk and will be passed to the baby, more with Depo Provera than with Noristerat. Research looking at the health and development of children hasn't produced any evidence of harm, but long-term research (into what might happen when the children are in their teens and beyond) has not been done.

Cancer

Much of the debate about injectables has centred on the possibility of the increased risk of cancer, particularly of the breast and the uterus. Studies on animals have shown an increased risk of both of these when large doses of Depo Provera are given for many years. Controversy centres on whether it's actually possible to compare the specific animals used (beagle dogs, rats and monkeys) with humans, as well as on whether it's reasonable to suggest that the effect of such high doses will be the same if lower doses are used.

One can't help feeling that if the results of these animal studies had been more reassuring doctors and licensing bodies would have been quite happy to think them relevant to women. Researchers usually defend their use of animals by saying the results *are* meaningful in the development of drugs for humans. Now they are saying that beagles are particularly vulnerable to bad effects from hormones, and that rats and monkeys have metabolisms that can't be compared with that of the human.

There has yet to be definitive research results on the links between cancer and Depo Provera in women. An interim report of a World Health Organisation study on Depo Provera has suggested there might be a risk of cervical cancer that increases the longer you are on the drug, but the research project has yet to publish its final results.

Hormonal implants and rings

Contraceptive implants are the longest lasting method of hormonal contraception currently available. Small capsules are placed under the skin, and then release *progestogen* for five years at a time.

Marketed as Norplant, this new system has been undergoing research trials since 1975, and is likely to be available in this country from 1988 onwards. The kind of progestogen used is levonorgestrol, the same chemical used in some progestogen-only pills. Norplant is therefore very similar to the POP, but because the implants release a constant and consistent dose of the hormone, less is needed to produce the contraceptive effect. And because the release of the drug is constant there aren't the fluctuations in hormone levels that happen when you're taking the POP, and this is thought to make Norplant more reliable as a contraceptive than the progestogen-only pill – around 99 per cent.

Norplant's effects on the body are very similar to those of the POP, so you should read this section in conjunction with the one on progestogen-only pills (see page 133) if you are considering using the method. The way it works as a contraceptive is thought to be the same as the POP. Cervical mucus is thickened so that it's difficult for sperm to penetrate, and ovulation may also be prevented. The lining of the uterus is changed too, so that it doesn't allow the implantation of a fertilised egg.

The progestogen is contained in six small capsules, 2.4mm in diameter and 34mm long. The capsules are made of a synthetic material, silastic, which enables the slow release of progestogen over the following five years.

The doctor will probably prefer to insert them during the first seven days of the menstrual cycle when it is unlikely that you could be already pregnant. They are inserted under the skin of the upper arm or forearm through tiny incisions which should heal quickly. You will have a mild local anaesthetic before the incisions are made. There is no need for the skin to be stitched afterwards because the incisions are so small.

Just as with the POP it is very likely that your menstrual cycle will be disturbed. You could stop having periods altogether, or find they become very irregular. There may also be some spotting between periods. Irregularity is most likely to happen during the first year of using Norplant, with a gradual decrease in menstrual problems thereafter.

Norplant can be removed at any time, and there is no evidence of any long-term effect on fertility once you are off it. There may be some delay in the return of your usual menstrual cycle, but research has shown that after a slight delay the pregnancy rates of women who have used Norplant are the same as those who have not used any hormonal contraception – nearly 80 per cent of those who used it are pregnant within a year, and 90 per cent within two years.

If you do get pregnant whilst using Norplant there is probably the same increased risk of ectopic pregnancy (see page 138) as there is with the progestogen-only pill. If you use it when you're breast-feeding a small amount of the hormone is likely to be transmitted to your baby (see page 139), and it is not known what effects this may have, if any.

Norplant may be a good option if you want long-term contraception, but don't want to get sterilised at this point. The major advantage over the POP is that you don't have to remember to take it at the same time every day, and its effectiveness is not dependent on your remembering to take it. It appears to have fewer negative effects than injectable progestogens (Depo Provera and Noristerat), which produce very high levels of hormones when they are first injected. It is not known whether Norplant has any specific long-term effects that differ from other forms of progestogen-only contraception, because there has not been enough time for any long-term research, and not enough women have used it.

Other forms of hormonal implants are also being investigated at the moment. A two-capsule system is being researched, as is a one-capsule version, which would act as a contraceptive for around 18 months.

Progestogen-releasing vaginal rings

The vaginal ring is yet another way of delivering progestogen into the body. It is about 50mm in diameter and about 8mm thick (smaller than a diaphragm). It is made of silastic, just like Norplant, which alows the slow release of the chemical in the core of the ring. The type of progestogen used is levonorgestrel. This is absorbed through the surface of the vagina into the bloodstream. Once the hormone has been absorbed the contraceptive effect is achieved in the same way as Norplant and the progestogen-only pill (see page 134). The ring is worn more or less constantly for three months, but can be removed when you have intercourse. It should be reinserted after intercourse.

The vaginal ring releases less hormone into your body than Norplant or the POP, so it is thought that its bad effects are less. But this lower level of hormone also makes the ring slightly less reliable than Norplant – about 98 per cent. Menstrual irregularity is also common.

There have been reports that the vaginal ring can cause irritation to the vagina, as well as increased discharge and a bad smell. The implications of these symptoms and effects on the vagina and cervix are not known, as there has not been any long-term research on the effects of the ring. Expulsion of the ring has also been reported. This would not decrease its efficiency as a contraceptive, but would be inconvenient as you'd have to reinsert it every time.

Once you stop using the ring, fertility should return in the same way as it does following the POP or Norplant (see page 139).

Research is also under way into a vaginal ring which releases both oestrogen and progestogen, just like the combined pill. So far there have been problems with some of its effects, which include an unpleasant discharge and frequent breakthrough bleeding. The combined ring would be worn three weeks out of four, with a withdrawal bleed during the week you don't wear it.

10

INTRA-UTERINE DEVICES

Reliability rate 96-98 per cent

It has been known since the middle of the last century that the introduction of a foreign body into a woman's uterus will prevent pregnancy. Though it was known that pregnancy in animals (notably camels) could be prevented this way, it wasn't until 'stem pessaries' made of gold, silver or wood were used to 'regulate' menstruation that their contraceptive action in women became obvious.

More sophisticated devices were designed in the early part of this century, but were rejected by a medical profession which was frequently hostile to contraception. The idea was pursued further in the 1920s and '30s, but only by a few researchers. Devices made of synthetic material were researched in Japan in the 1950s, after which further research followed in the 1960s in America. The designs produced then are the basis of what is now available.

The first designs of these intra-uterine devices (IUDs) are still in use today; flexible plastic devices which can be inserted into the uterus without needing to dilate the cervix. These were first used by women who had given birth, since it was difficult to fit them in those who hadn't – they were too big. The introduction of smaller IUDs, wound with copper wire, followed in the early 1970s. Because of their size these could be fitted in women who had not had children, and are now the ones almost exclusively used.

How the IUD prevents pregnancy

Although it is not exactly clear how IUDs work, as time goes on the possibilities have narrowed. It is generally agreed that the IUD can stop *an already fertilised egg* from implanting itself into the lining of the uterus. This is because the presence of a foreign body (the IUD) causes a change in the biological environment, possibly an increase in the proportion of white blood cells. These are able to prevent implantation, and may also inactivate sperm. The copper wire around the IUD also has a mildly spermicidal effect. These factors put together achieve a reliability rate of up to 98 per cent.

The fact that the IUD has the effect of not allowing implantation (resulting in the death of the fertilised egg) may be especially important to you, because it means it causes a very early abortion of a several days' old embryo. Depending on your moral or religious beliefs this could make the method unacceptable.

Who can use the IUD?

The IUD is most suitable for a woman in a monogamous sexual relationship who is unlikely to get a sexually transmitted disease. She should also be prepared to risk the slight chance of problems that could make it more difficult to have children in future years.

Although the newer, smaller IUDs can be fitted in young women who have not had children, they are no longer promoted as a 'first choice' method for these women. But this has nothing to do with either age or childbirth, but with sex. Regardless of your age, if you have frequent sex with more than one partner, or your partner has sex with someone else as well as you, the risk of infection is increased. The IUD increases the risk of *transmission* of this infection, and so makes it more likely that you'll get it.

Serious pelvic inflammatory disease (PID) can follow, and this can result in damage to the reproductive system, especially to the delicate fallopian tubes, which could mean it is impossible to get pregnant at a later date.

Older women who have had children are likely to be offered the IUD. Doctors assume that this group of women will have a stable and monogamous sexual relationship, and are therefore less at risk. It is further assumed that infertility is unlikely to be a great worry for those who have had children – they may have completed their families anyway, so not being able to have more children wouldn't be a disaster.

But if you are, for instance, 33 years old with two children, and you are sexually active with more than one partner, using an IUD could mean your fertility is at risk. It may be very important to you that you don't jeopardise it. And even if you are 22 with no children and in a monogamous long-term relationship, the comparatively smaller risk of PID still may mean you don't want to use the method.

The effects of the IUD, including the risk of infection, will be discussed later and in more detail. But if you are an older woman with children, you should know from the outset that these two elements don't in themselves make the method physically safer, even if this is what your doctor appears to base her or his judgement on when you are offered the method. It's yet another example of the way in which health information is given to women – thought to be 'for our own good' but missing out vital parts of the equation.

The IUD can cause painful and heavy periods in any woman, as well as an increase in the risk of pelvic inflammatory disease. If you have a disability that means you lack sensation in your abdomen you might not be able to tell that you have PID, since pain is the major symptom. It could also be hard to tell whether you have an ectopic pregnancy (see page 164). Both PID and ectopic pregnancy are likely to be accompanied by other symptoms, so you should keep a check on these and report anything unusual to your doctor. Lack of sensation in your fingers and lack of manual dexterity could make it difficult for you to check that the IUD is in place (see page 161). Instead your partner can learn to check it for you.

For those whom it suits, the IUD can be a remarkably trouble-free form of contraception. You can have sexual intercourse whenever you wish without having to think about contraception, indeed you don't have to remember to do anything except to check it's in place once a month and go to the doctor for a yearly check-up. And it's a very reliable form of contraception.

But as one jolly (male) gynaecologist puts it, 'When it is good it is very very good, but when it is bad it is horrid.' The problems that can occur with an IUD may be very unpleasant, and can pose a risk to later fertility. Even though you may not be in the high risk group for these problems, everyone using the method faces some increase of that risk.

Types of IUD

Lippes loop This IUD was the one most widely used for many years. Made of polythene, it comes in four sizes and can be left in place for five years or more – indefinitely if there are no problems. It is easier to insert in women who have had children.

Saf-T-Coil Made of a type of vinyl, this device is no longer marketed (for commercial reasons – it is as safe and effective as any other device). It can be left in place indefinitely if there are no problems.

Copper 7 (Gravigard) A plastic device, it is shaped like a '7', with the stem wound with fine copper wire. The mini Copper 7 is also used by women with smaller uteruses. Both of these devices can be left in place for two years. The Copper 7 was withdrawn from sale in America in 1986 because it was the subject of so many lawsuits by women who had problems with it that the manufacturers decided that production was no longer an economic proposition. Now manufacture of these devices has stopped in the UK too. There is no evidence that there are any more risks associated with this design of IUD than with any other, so there is no need to have it removed if you had one inserted less than two years ago. But you would have to change to another kind of IUD if you want to have a new one inserted once the two years are up.

Copper T (Ortho-Gyne T) This is plastic, with the stem wound with copper wire. It can be left in place for three years.

Ortho-Gyne T 380 slimline Similar to the above, but with more copper wire. It can be left in place for four years.

Multiload Cu 250 This device is also manufactured in a smaller size. It is wound with copper, and the little protrusions on the arms are designed to hold it in place inside the uterus. It can be left in place for three years.

Novagard and **Nova T** These are two identical devices made by different manufacturers. They are plastic, and wound with copper wire. The wire has a core made of silver which means it will last

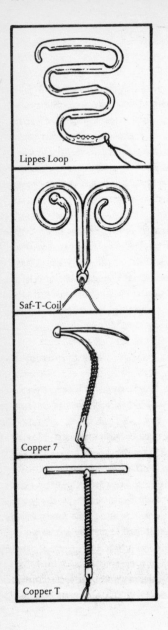

Lippes Loop

Saf-T-Coil

Copper 7

Copper T

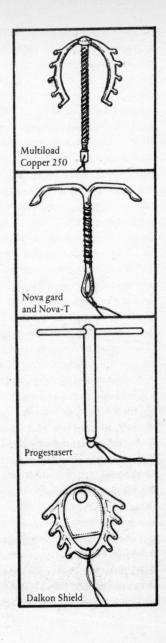

Multiload
Copper 250

Nova gard
and Nova-T

Progestasert

Dalkon Shield

glonger – about five years. The devices are also comparatively small.

Progestasert This is impregnated with the natural hormone progesterone, and it is thought to be a good IUD for women with heavy and painful periods who otherwise could not use one. It was supposed to help menstrual problems. The Progestasert is not promoted in this country, but can be obtained on private prescription from some doctors. It is left in place for one year only; research continues into developing a similar device that has a longer life.

Dalkon Shield This design of IUD was found to cause serious problems, especially for women who got pregnant whilst using it. The construction of the multi-filament tail is thought to have encouraged the transmission of infection to the uterus, increasing the risk of septic (infected) miscarriage and other types of infection too. The design was withdrawn in 1975, but it is thought that there may still be women who are fitted with the device. If you are fitted with a Dalkon Shield (or know anyone who is), it should be removed, or you should have a check-up if you haven't had your IUD checked for many years and don't know what it is.

Having an IUD fitted

IUD fitting takes skill and experience. It's best to have it fitted by a trained family planning doctor, who fits IUDs frequently. A GP who fits only a few a year may not be so good at doing it. So either go to the local family planning clinic, or check with your GP on her training and how often she fits the device.

The fitting should be preceded by a discussion of your medical history, current lifestyle and health. If you suffer or have suffered from any of the following an IUD may not be suitable:

● pelvic inflammatory disease (PID), now or in the past six months
● very heavy and/or painful periods
● a recent septic abortion (infection after the operation)
● polyps or fibroids in your uterus
● an abnormally formed uterus
● cancer of the cervix or uterus, or abnormal cervical smear results

- endometriosis
- blood disorders
- anaemia
- heart disease
- kidney disease
- gonorrhea
- allergy to copper (makes a copper-containing IUD unsuitable)

Diabetes and the taking of steroid drugs do not increase the health risks of an IUD but could lessen its reliability because these may change the uterine environment.

Most doctors will not fit an IUD in a woman who is under 20 and who has not had children, unless no other contraceptive can be used.

You should be shown an IUD, preferably in conjunction with a model of the uterus and cervix so you can see how it will be fitted. You should also be told how to check your IUD is still in place, as well as about danger signs after IUD insertion which mean you should return to your doctor (see page 162).

Some doctors prefer to insert the IUD towards the end of your period. It may be slightly easier to insert it through the softer post-menstrual cervix, but it is mainly so that they can be sure you are not already pregnant. It is also because you won't notice any slight bleeding caused by the insertion because it will be mixed with menstrual blood. But there is no evidence that the IUD is more reliable when it's inserted at this time, and you could land up getting pregnant during the time you're waiting to go back to the doctor for insertion. If you have had sex without contraception in the previous five days the IUD will have a post-coital contraceptive effect (see below), so it can be fitted and be effective in preventing pregnancy up to day 19 of your menstrual cycle.

You may also be offered an IUD immediately after childbirth or abortion. The risk of expulsion is greater after childbirth, so it's probably worth waiting until six weeks or so after the birth to have an IUD fitted.

Post-coital IUD – insertion after you've had sex without contraception

An IUD can be inserted up to five days after you have had sex without contraception and risked pregnancy. The IUD prevents implantation of any fertilised egg, so if you have conceived, the pregnancy won't continue. This amounts to a very early abortion, so if you have moral or religious objections to abortion you may not want to use this method.

The doctor should check that it's okay for you to use the IUD, and that you have no health problems that could increase the risk of infection or ectopic pregnancy. It is only worth using the IUD post-coitally if you plan to continue with it as a method of contraception in the long term. The advantages and disadvantages of the IUD inserted after sex are the same as when it is inserted at any other time.

IUD insertion – what happens

You will lie on the doctor's examination couch, your legs apart as they are for an internal examination. The doctor should first examine you, and check the position of your uterus and cervix.

She will the insert a speculum, which separates your vaginal walls making it easier to see and gain access to the cervix. The cervix will then be held by an instrument called a tentaculum, which keeps the cervix in line with the uterus. This reduces the risk of bleeding and perforation of the uterus. It may feel uncomfortable, but is especially important if your cervix is difficult to reach.

The size and position of your uterus and cervical canal will then be gauged with a *uterine sound*. The doctor can then work out what size of IUD you should have, and also whether your cervical canal is obstructed in some way so that an IUD can't be fitted.

The uterine sound is then withdrawn, and the *introducer tube* inserted into the cervical canal. The IUD itself is inserted through the introducer. It regains its shape as soon as it is in place in the uterus.

The inserter tube and tentaculum are then withdrawn, and the strings of the IUD are trimmed.

Pain on IUD insertion

You may well experience pain during and immediately after IUD insertion, especially if you have not had children and your cervical opening is tight. Cramps similar to period pain may follow, and might last for hours or a few days. You can minimise this pain by taking aspirin *before* insertion. Aspirin has been found to work particularly effectively with this kind of pain.

Relaxation during insertion is very important. The relationship you have with your doctor will make a considerable difference to this – if you feel confident and well informed you are likely to be more relaxed. It's worth having a supportive friend with you when you are fitted, who can take you home afterwards. You may want to rest for a while before leaving the clinic to let the cramps subside.

Some doctors will use a local anaesthetic in your cervix if you cannot stand the pain. A few will be prepared to give you a general anaesthetic, but most would think the risks of a general anaesthetic aren't worth taking for the sake of having an IUD. If you are very worried about insertion you might be better off considering another method of contraception.

If the pain is intolerable during an IUD fitting you must tell the doctor immediately, who can stop the insertion if it's not already too advanced.

Problems during insertion

● **Perforation of the uterus** is a rare complication of IUD insertion, and is likely to cause severe pain. Doctors with skill and experience with IUD insertion cause fewer perforations.

● **Fainting during insertion** can be linked to tension and anxiety about it, as well as pain. This can make you breathe too fast and too deeply, which can make you feel faint.

After insertion

You should have already been told what kind of IUD you've got, and how to check the strings. You should also have been told that the first couple of periods after insertion are likely to be heavier and more painful, but that this should improve after a few cycles.

You should make an appointment for a check-up within three months of insertion, and not before you have had at least one full menstrual cycle and a period. You can use tampons with an IUD.

There may be a small amount of bleeding immediately after insertion (which you won't notice if you are already having a period), but this should stop within a few days. Sometimes there is a little mid-cycle bleeding in the first few cycles as your uterus gets used to having the IUD inside it.

It's difficult to specify at what point any of the above could necessitate a return visit to your doctor before the planned check-up, but if you are in any doubt you should return to the doctor who fitted the device. If the doctor thinks the problem is within normal limits, she will probably suggest you wait and see what happens, and tell you that it is likely to lessen over the next few months. If you are having very heavy periods you may need iron tablets, so go back to your doctor if the second period after IUD insertion is very heavy.

If your sexual partner complains about the threads of the IUD sticking into his penis when you have intercourse, the threads may have been cut too short. If the threads *suddenly* get too short the IUD may have moved up inside the uterus, so it is important to get the device checked.

How to check your IUD

Because expulsion of an IUD is most likely to happen during a period, you should check that it's in place immediately after menstruation.

Put one or two fingers inside your vagina and feel for your cervix. You can use your middle finger or the middle and first fingers. Your cervix is firm and round, and feels a bit like the end of your nose. Gently move your finger over the surface. You'll probably be able to feel the dimple in the middle which is the entrance to the cervical canal. The threads (or thread) extend out of the opening, and will be about 2in (5cm) long, and made of fine nylon. If they are longer than this they might have wrapped themselves around the cervix. This is fine, as long as you can feel them coming out of the cervical opening as they should.

If you cannot feel the threads, or if you can feel the plastic stem of the IUD protruding through the cervical opening, return to the doctor immediately. The device may not be properly in place.

IUD danger signs
Go back to the doctor if you experience any of the following:

- severe cramps or pain in the abdomen
- high temperature or fever
- late period, no period, or a very light period
- pain after an unusually light period
- unusual mid-cycle bleeding
- unusual vaginal discharge, maybe with a bad smell
- pain during or after intercourse
- bleeding during or after intercourse

All of these warnings apply throughout the time you have an IUD – not only during the first few months. Pain and fever could be caused by an internal infection, pain after a light period could be a symptom of an ectopic pregnancy. Both of these are dangerous and need immediate treatment (see page 164).

Physical problems associated with having an IUD

Women who have an IUD have an increased risk of getting pelvic inflammatory disease (PID), which is an infection of the uterus, fallopian tubes or ovaries. The risk for an IUD user is around twice that of a woman using barrier methods or the pill.

PID incidence and contraceptive use

method	PID incidence per 1,000 women
IUD	52
no method	34
barrier method	14
pill	9

The table shows that pill and barrier method users actually have a reduced risk of PID, and that IUD users run a greater risk of it than those not using contraception.

PID is caused when bacteria move up from the vagina, through the cervical opening and into the uterus and fallopian tubes. It is not entirely clear why IUD users run an increased risk. The fact that bacteria can travel up IUD threads and into the uterus is probably the main reason, but it could also be because the changes to the uterine lining caused by the device increase vulnerability to infection, or because women with IUDs have longer and heavier periods during which they are more vulnerable to infection. None of these has been conclusively confirmed, and no one has found a way of minimising this risk. Most studies comparing IUDs with and without threads did not show that one was better than the other.

There is one additional cause which has been confirmed: bacteria entering the vagina at the time of insertion. This risk can be decreased by better and more hygienic insertion techniques. Research continues into disinfectants that can be used to clean the IUD before insertion, or which can be impregnated into the threads of the device. This may be the reason why there is a higher rate of PID during the first month after insertion, which diminishes with duration of use. IUD insertion can also cause a pre-existing infection to flare up again and cause PID.

Pelvic inflammatory disease in women who don't use IUDs is usually caused by sexually transmitted diseases, particularly chlamydia and gonorrhea. If you are an IUD user, with an already increased risk of PID, and then get a sexually transmitted disease, the risk is obviously increased. Women who have more than one sexual partner, or who have frequent sex with just one partner, run a greater risk of getting sexually transmitted disease.

Some doctors will give you antibiotics and remove the IUD if you get PID. Others remove the device only if the antibiotics don't work quickly. There is no evidence which is the better approach in the long term, but antibiotics *must* be given regardless of whether or not the IUD is removed.

Actinomycosis

The actinomyces organism is more often found in IUD users than in non-users. In many women it doesn't produce any symptoms, but some will develop actinomycosis, a kind of fungal infection of the reproductive organs. The severity of this varies. It is treated with antibiotics, and the device should be removed. Even in those cases where there are no symptoms some doctors will remove the IUD. You should certainly be closely monitored if actinomyces organisms are detected, even if you have no symptoms at this stage.

The IUD and pregnancy

● **Ectopic pregnancy**, when a fertilised egg implants itself outside the uterus (usually in a fallopian tube), is more likely in IUD users. Between one in 20 to one in 30 pregnancies in IUD users are ectopic, compared to one in 200 pregnancies in non-IUD users. The hostile environment created by the IUD does not extend to the fallopian tubes, and there may even be changes in the tubes caused by the IUD which encourage an ectopic pregnancy, especially if there is an IUD-related infection in them.

But it is difficult to draw definite conclusions about why the risk of an ectopic pregnancy is increased. Both the pill and barrier methods lower the chance of an ectopic pregnancy, but it is not known what risk is run by women who have never used any contraception. PID increases the risk of an ectopic pregnancy, and since PID is more common in IUD users this could be a major factor in the increased incidence.

An ectopic pregnancy will have to be surgically removed, and usually means the loss of the fallopian tube. This may well have an effect on later fertility, even if the remaining fallopian tube is intact and healthy.

It is therefore vital that you see your doctor immediately if you develop any of the symptoms of ectopic pregnancy – abdominal pain, a light period maybe with dark brownish blood or a missed period, especially followed by pain. This pain may be concentrated on one side of your lower abdomen.

The likelihood of ectopic pregnancy increases the longer you use an IUD, and remains slightly higher after removal – if you have used an IUD for two years or more there is a slightly increased risk of an ectopic pregnancy for the year following removal than if you had never had the device.

● **Uterine pregnancy**, with an IUD in place, increases the risk of miscarriage. About half of all IUD pregnancies will spontaneously abort during the first two trimesters of pregnancy. This risk is reduced if the device is removed, but may still threaten the pregnancy during the first trimester.

Sometimes, because of uterine changes that happen in pregnancy, the device will rise a little so that the strings are no longer visible, and it therefore cannot be removed without risking the pregnancy. If you want to continue the pregnancy you will need to be closely monitored because of the risk of miscarriage and/or infection. If the IUD remains in place throughout the pregnancy there is a higher risk of the baby being born premature, or with a low birth weight. There is no evidence at all for an increased risk of any foetal abnormality, either if the device was present at the time of conception or left in during pregnancy. This applies to all IUDs.

Painful and heavy periods

This is the most commonly experienced disadvantage of the IUD. Your periods may be heavier, last longer, and be more painful. 'Inert' IUDs like the Lippes loop seem to be particularly associated with menstrual problems – the smaller copper devices are thought to be better.

This may improve after the first few cycles, but you may find it intolerable before that time and want the IUD removed. You may also find the problem continues, and may want the device removed, say, after six months.

It may be that the IUD has been incorrectly fitted, or is simply too big. An X-ray or ultrasonic scan could confirm whether this is the case. If it is, you should have the device removed, and have a smaller device or try a different method of contraception.

If you had heavy or painful periods before the IUD was fitted, it may make them worse.

The IUD and long-term use

Assuming you have had no problems already, you should have a check-up within the first three months after insertion, and then once a year. The IUD should be removed in accordance with the manufacturer's recommended length of use (which for the copper IUDs will be from two to five years).

Removal of the IUD in the middle of your menstrual cycle could allow the implantation of an already fertilised egg, so if you want to avoid pregnancy the IUD should be removed either during or immediately before a period.

Removal is usually a lot less painful than insertion. The method is similar (see page 159), but in reverse. You can have a new IUD fitted immediately if you wish.

11

STERILISATION

Sterilisation has become an increasingly popular option since the beginning of the 1970s. More and more people every year decide to take this major step which will mean they can no longer have children. An estimated 60,000 couples in England and Wales now rely on either vasectomy or female sterilisation, and this total grows every year. Figures show that in 1970 only 4 per cent of all those of reproductive age had been sterilised. By 1983-84 the proportion stood at 22 per cent.

There are many reasons for this increase. Technical advances have meant that sterilisation operations are easier and safer. Both vasectomy and female sterilisation are available free on the National Health Service – though waiting lists can be long – and both operations are done for a reasonable fee and minimal waiting time by the charitable health sector.

A change in attitudes to contraception must also be partly responsible for the increase. Female sterilisation is most common among women in their mid to late thirties who don't want any more pregnancies but who also don't want to continue for what may be two or more decades with the pill, IUD or barrier method. Sterilisation deals with contraception once and for all, and is more reliable than any other method.

Men's sense of responsibility in relation to sexuality and contraception has also changed. More men feel that it's time they should take their turn in the form of some practical step to prevent conception, and vasectomy is no longer seen as a kind of castration, with the destruction of sexual identity that implies. Vasectomy is a much simpler operation than female sterilisation. This may be a deciding factor if both you and your partner are willing to be sterilised.

Sterilisation is usually thought of as an option for those who 'have completed their families', who are in a stable monogamous relationship and don't want any more children. It is very difficult to get a doctor to do the operation if you don't fit into this bracket, especially if you're young and have decided you never want to have children. Looking at research into the psychological effects of sterilisation it's easy to see why – both regret and requests for sterilisation reversal (see page 178) are far more likely in those who had the operation when young.

Ideally, sterilisation should be done only when you've had time to consider the decision away from the context of other major decisions or events in your life. You would therefore be better off not having it done at the same time as an abortion or childbirth, when there is more chance of both physical and emotional problems as a result of the operation. Female sterilisation immediately after childbirth is more likely to result in post-operative problems, and in a higher failure rate.

The decision to be sterilised should not be made under pressure – either from your doctor or partner. The medical profession has just about realised this, and the number of sterilisations done at the same time as abortion or childbirth has begun to drop. There has been evidence that some doctors have used sterilisation as a condition of abortion if, for example, they thought the woman concerned was 'irresponsible' and likely to have more unplanned and unwanted pregnancies, or if she was young, poor, and already had children. Women with disabilities may also be pressurised to have a sterilisation operation, on the assumption that they could not manage other forms of contraception, or that they have no right to choose whether or not to have children. Doctors have no right to set such conditions, and you should not consent to anything that you don't want, and at a time you don't want it.

Pressure can also come from your own feelings about abortion or childbirth. At one particular time you may feel there is no way you could want or face another pregnancy, and that you must take immediate action to stop any future possibility of it. But once the crisis is over your feelings could change completely, and however difficult it is, you should take this into account. What are the implications of waiting for a few months until you have the sterilisation operation? It may well be that you don't change your mind, but you will have the opportunity to make the decision at your own pace, and not have it accelerated by the force of current circumstance.

But, in the end, regardless of what is happening when you decide to be sterilised, it is impossible to predict exactly what your life will be like in the future, and whether anything could happen that could make you change your mind about having had the operation. You may be in a very different kind of sexual relationship five years from now, or your feelings within your current relationship could change considerably. The chance of a successful sterilisation reversal (see page 174) is not high – less than 60 per cent for women, and less than 30 per cent for men. Given this, your decision to have the operation has to be based on the assumption that it is irreversible, and you should be sure as you possibly can be that you won't regret it and want it reversed.

Making up your mind – counselling

Recent research asking people how they made the decision to be sterilised has shown that formal and professional counselling isn't always vital, but should be available. Most people make the decision together with their sexual partner, as well as discussing it with friends and relations. By the time you actually make the request to have the operation, and discuss it with a doctor or counsellor, you may well be very sure it's what you want. But discussion with someone you don't know, and who isn't closely emotionally involved with the decision, can be very useful. It gives you a chance to reflect on your own reasons for sterilisation, and to hear what they sound like when you put them forward. You'll also be able to find out more about the operation itself.

The doctor or counsellor may question you quite closely to see whether you've thought about the implications of the decision. Depending on the approach of the professional concerned, this may or may not be helpful. If you feel that you have to prove a case, rather than explore your own feelings and attitudes, you may not get much out of it.

Most doctors will want confirmation that your partner has agreed to your having the operation, but this is not a legal requirement. You may find it difficult to get a sterilisation operation if you are not in a stable relationship, but this is a question of the doctor's decision, not the law.

How it's done — female sterilisation

Failure rate: one in 300

There are a number of different techniques used to perform female sterilisation. Most doctors now prefer to do either a laparoscopy or a mini-laparotomy (see below). Both of these are simpler to do than other techniques, require much smaller incisions in the abdominal wall, and involve less recovery time and a shorter stay in hospital. It's best to have the operation either during a period or immediately afterwards, so you can be sure you are not already pregnant. If you are on the pill you can take it as usual right up until the day of the operation.

Laparoscopy

This technique involves making two small incisions in your abdomen and can be done under either local or general anaesthetic. The upper incision (near your navel) is for the introduction of a *laparoscope* which is a tube with a light at the end, through which the doctor can see inside you. Before the laparoscope is introduced, the doctor will use this incision to pump gas (carbon dioxide or nitrous oxide) into your abdomen. This makes the abdominal wall rise up away from your internal organs, so that a space is created in which the doctor can see the fallopian tubes and operate on them.

The second incision is made just above your pubic hair line, directly above the fallopian tubes. Once the doctor has access to the tubes, sterilisation can be done in a number of ways:

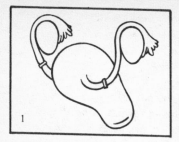

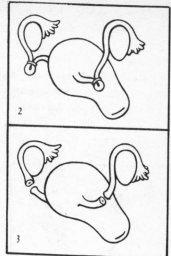

1 A plastic clip ½-1in (1-2cm) long is put on each fallopian tube to prevent eggs moving down towards the uterus and sperm going up them

2 Each tube is looped and the loop secured with a silastic ring

3 Each tube is divided and sealed using *diathermy*, which is like a tiny burn

After the operation, the surgical instruments are withdrawn and the two abdominal incisions closed with a few stitches or little clips. They should heal within a fortnight.

You may feel very uncomfortable after the operation because of the gas that still remains inside your abdomen. This should disperse after a day, but until it does it may cause pain both in your abdomen and shoulders. There may also be some pain and bruising around the abdominal incisions. This may persist for a fortnight or so.

Depending on the routine of the place where you had the operation, you will go home after 24 hours, or earlier. Many clinics in the charitable sector let you go home the same day. Take it very easy for the next two days. You should not do any heavy physical work for a week. If your job isn't physically demanding you can return within a day or so of the operation. You can have intercourse as soon as you want to, and the operation is reliable immediately so there is no need for contraception.

Your first period after the operation may be a bit late, particularly if the operation was done in the second half of the cycle. You should return to the doctor for a check-up after six weeks.

Laparotomy

A laparotomy involves a much larger incision in the abdomen than a laparoscopy, because a laparoscope is not used. The operation is done under general anaesthetic. The doctor has to be able to see both fallopian tubes, on which she or he then performs *tubal ligation* (literally 'tying up' the tubes). This can be done by:

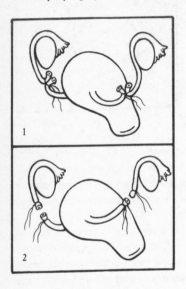

1 looping each tube, tying the loops with a dissolvable thread, and then cutting the tubes. Once the stitch has dissolved the two ends of the tube will separate

2 cutting the tube, separating the cut ends and putting a dissolvable stitch between each end

cutting out a section of fallopian tube. The ends nearest the ovaries are folded backwards so the tubes can't rejoin

crushing and tying up each tube with a non-dissolvable thread

Because this is a more major operation you will have to stay in hospital for a few days. There may also be more post-operative pain from which it takes longer to recover. Laparotomy is often the method chosen after childbirth, particularly if the birth is a Caesarian and an incision has already been made.

Mini-laparotomy

The sterilisation techniques used in a mini-laparotomy are the same as in an ordinary laparotomy, but the abdominal incision is much smaller. The incision is made just above the pubic hair line, or higher. The doctor then uses a *uterine elevator* put into your vagina, which moves the uterus upwards and the fallopian tubes to just below the incision so that the doctor can have direct access to them.

You would be able to go home within one or two days of a mini-laparotomy. The incision should heal within three weeks – don't do any heavy physical work (including lifting) until after the three weeks. If your job doesn't involve physical strain you will probably be able to go back to work three or four days after the operation.

Other female sterilisation techniques

The techniques described above are now the most widely used, as they are simpler to do, have a low complication rate and don't involve a long stay in hospital. Few doctors now do *total salpingectomy* (complete removal of the fallopian tubes), because more complications are likely to follow. Other routes apart from the abdominal wall through which to insert the laparoscope are not used much now. In the past they included *culdoscopy* (inserting the laparoscope in the vagina) and *hysteroscopy* (inserting it through the uterus). Culdoscopy is still performed sometimes, particularly in America, but it is clear that complications are more frequent with this method. *Hysterectomy* (complete removal of the uterus) *should never be done solely for the purpose of sterilisation*.

Return to your doctor if you have severe pain anywhere in the abdomen after sterilisation, or pain accompanied by a raised temperature. This could indicate an infection, or that some other internal organ has been damaged during the operation. Return also if there is any bleeding – immediately if the bleeding is heavy. You might be haemorrhaging. Complications of this sort are very rare.

Who can't have female sterilisation

If you suffer from any condition which makes it dangerous for you to have surgery you may have to avoid sterilisation – discuss this with your doctor.

If you have already had a lot of abdominal surgery, for whatever reason, this too may make the operation inadvisable.

If you are very overweight it may be difficult for the doctor to perform the operation because of the amount of fat over the abdominal wall itself, making it difficult to get the surgical instruments far enough into the abdominal cavity.

After female sterilisation

You should be fully recovered within days or weeks of the operation, depending on which technique was used. You may find that your next period is a bit late.

There have been suggestions that periods are likely to be heavier and more painful following sterilisation. Research done in Britain, as part of a World Health Organisation study on the effects of sterilisation, did find that those who had been sterilised with the diathermy technique were more likely to experience shorter cycles and heavier periods, but it is not yet clear why this might be. This does not appear to be a problem with clip or ring sterilisation. Some researchers have suggested that this could be related to the kind of contraceptive you used before the operation, but more research is needed into this. Certainly if you were previously on the pill your periods are likely to be heavier and more painful once you are sterilised and off it, because you will now be having a menstrual cycle instead of a pill cycle.

Though the failure rate for female sterilisation is low, any pregnancies that do occur are more likely to be ectopic (see page 164) because the fertilised egg won't be able to travel down the fallopian tube into the uterus. If you have any pain of the kind associated with an ectopic pregnancy you should see a doctor as soon as possible.

Reversal of female sterilisation

The average success rate for sterilisation reversal is around 60 per cent, but this will depend both on the skill of the surgeon doing the reversal and the sterilisation technique originally used. Techniques that don't involve much destruction of the fallopian tubes are easier to reverse, so you have a better chance of successful reversal if your sterilisation method used clips, rings, or only a small amount of fallopian tube being removed or repositioned if you had tubal ligation.

You will have to have a laparotomy to enable the doctor to put the tubes back together again. The damaged part of the tube will be removed, and the undamaged ends of the tubes rejoined. There still may be a higher risk of ectopic pregnancy following a reversal because the tubes may remain slightly damaged.

Vasectomy

Failure rate: one in 1,000

Vasectomy is now widely available – your GP can refer you for an NHS vasectomy which is free, but you may find there is a long waiting list. Many agencies in the charitable private health sector offer vasectomy at a reasonable price and with the minimum of wait once you've made up your mind. The operation is almost always done on a day-care basis, so you'll be able to go home the same day.

You will probably be told to shave or cut the pubic hair from your testicles and around your penis before you have the operation. No other preparation need be made.

How it's done

Vasectomy is normally done with a local anaesthetic. This is injected into the tissue of and around the *vas deferens* which is the tube that leads from your testes to the penis.

The doctor will then make a small incision just above the vas deferens, which lies very near to the skin surface. The technique used to perform the vasectomy itself varies, depending on the doctor's preference. The tube may be divided, and the ends cauterised with a heated instrument so they are sealed, or divided and tied with undissolvable thread. Alternatively, a section of the tube may be completely removed. Usually each end is then repositioned so that they are unlikely to rejoin. Sometimes they are *ligated*, which means they are not divided but tied with two pieces of undissolvable thread. The skin incisions are then stitched together again with dissolvable thread.

After the operation you will need to wear either a jockstrap or a pair of supportive underpants. Bring either of these with you so you can wear them when you leave the clinic or hospital. It's best to have your partner or a friend with you to take you home, as you are likely to experience pain and soreness as the anaesthetic wears off. Aspirin should help with this.

After vasectomy

Your testicles may well be swollen and uncomfortable for several days, and there may be some bruising. You should continue to wear underpants that provide good support throughout the next week or so, including at night. You should avoid heavy physical work (including lifting) for two or three days, which could mean you have to take time off from your job. If your job doesn't involve this you might feel okay about going back to work the day after the operation. If you take it easy, it is much less likely that you'll develop haematoma, which is a kind of solid bruise. This is very rare, but if it does happen you will have to rest until it subsides.

You should leave the dressings on the incisions for 24 hours. The dressings can then be removed. This is best done in the bath, as the warm water helps them to come off. As long as you continue to keep the area clean and dry no more dressings will be needed. The stitches on the incisions will gradually dissolve away over the next fortnight or so. You can have intercourse as soon as you and your partner wish, but you'll need to use contraception for at least the first three months (see below).

If you have any excessive swelling or pain, or the incisions continue to bleed, you should see your doctor immediately. Pain or swelling could mean infection, and bleeding could mean the incisions haven't been stitched up correctly, and may have to be done again.

Vasectomy takes some time to take effect, because you have to clear existing sperm from the tubes. It is thought to take between 24 and 36 ejaculations before you will be clear of sperm, so don't have intercourse without contraception until you have been told you are clear. The semen will look just as it did before regardless of whether or not it contains any sperm.

What usually happens is that you are asked to return to the clinic after three or four months with a sample of semen which can then be analysed to see if any sperm remain. You might be told immediately of the results, or you might be told a few days later by letter. If the sample contains any sperm you will have to return every month until the sample is pronounced clear. Once it has been clear for two samples running, you can have intercourse without contraception.

Very occasionally, the two cut or ligated ends of the vas deferens can rejoin and you will then be fertile again, hence the failure rate.

There is currently no evidence to suggest that vasectomy can cause any illness or other physical problem. There were suspicions that vasectomy could increase the risk of atherosclerosis (hardening of the arteries) and heart disease, following some research on vasectomised monkeys. The theory was that sperm, now unable to pass through the vas deferens, were affecting the level of fat in the blood. No research on humans has come up with such results, and large long-term studies continue without any further evidence appearing. Neither is there any evidence that vasectomy increases the risk of cancer.

There is evidence that your body may produce *sperm antibodies* after vasectomy. This doesn't happen in all men, and can happen even if you haven't been vasectomised. It may be a response to the presence of sperm that can no longer leave the body, and means the immune system is reacting against them and destroying them in various ways. There is no evidence at this point that sperm antibodies are associated with the increased likelihood of any illness or immunological problem. The production of sperm antibodies has been cited as one of the reasons why it is so difficult to do a successful reversal of the operation.

Vasectomy reversal

The success of vasectomy reversal depends very much on the skill and equipment of the surgeon, as well as the amount of damage to the vas deferens and the surrounding tissue the vasectomy involved. It's now possible to use microsurgical techniques, thought to be more successful because the cut tubes can be realigned much more precisely under a surgical microscope. The reversal operation will take a great deal longer to perform than the vasectomy did, and may be done under general anaesthetic.

Once you've had a reversal operation you should follow the post-operative routine described for vasectomy. You should be sexually abstinent (no masturbation or sex with your partner) for the next fortnight or month, after which you can have a semen sample analysed to see if it contains any sperm. This may not be back to normal for six months or more, but it varies. A few surgeons claim a reversal success rate of 85 per cent, but most others say it's far less.

The psychological effects of sterilisation for men and women

The evidence on psychological effects of sterilisation is clear and unsurprising. If you were clear about why you were having the operation, and were positive about the decision when you had the operation, you are very unlikely to experience any psychological problems as a result. Problems can occur if the decision was made under pressure, or as a response to a crisis.

Sterilisation (male or female) does not affect hormone levels, so it does not have any physiological effect on sexuality. There are no physical reasons why your libido (sex drive) should be lower than it was before the operation.

Some people have impossibly high expectations of sterilisation, and hope that it will solve all their relationship problems, make them enjoy sex more and be generally happier. Though the worry about pregnancy could mean that you feel more free about expressing yourself sexually there's no reason why it should restore mutual sexual attraction where little was there before, or solve other emotional difficulties between you and your partner.

If you, man or woman, had the operation under pressure from a doctor or anyone else, and not because you wanted it, you are much more likely to feel that your fertility has been stolen from you in some way, and yearn to have it back. Actually having another child may not be important to you, it's the sense of being fertile and with the potential for having children that counts. Your sense of your own sexuality may be very bound up with this, and you could find that you lose interest in sex now it has been separated from reproduction. Sterilisation reversal may seem the only way out of this, but you will have to remember that the success rate is not very high.

Research into why people regret sterilisation and seek reversals shows very clearly that if the operation is done at the same time as any other major life event – whether it be childbirth, abortion, financial wories, illness or relationship problems – it is much more likely to end in regret. You should therefore try to put off the decision if there is any crisis in your life, even though it may not appear to be directly related to the question of sterilisation. You can use contraception until the current problems have been resolved, and then take the time to discuss the decision with your partner or anyone else close to you, as well as with a doctor or counsellor once you have made the decision to seek the operation.

Even if it was a positive decision at the time, your circumstances can change so that you regret having had the operation. If you are separated from your previous partner and now in a new relationship you may find you want to have children. Once again, an attempted sterilisation reversal may be the only option.

12
ABORTION

Despite the advent of generally available contraception, there is still a need for abortion. Contraception can fail, and not every woman can use every method. Abortion is a vital back-up to current contraception, and its availability gives women the opportunity to have genuine control over their fertility.

The British abortion law has been under attack from the moment it came into force. The powerful anti-abortion lobby, led by religious and moral authoritarian activists, has done what it can to restrict the abortion law. Pro-choice campaigns have had to spend time defending the existing law, and have had little opportunity to press for improvements in abortion facilities. Whether you can get a safe, early abortion still depends on what part of the country you live in and the attitudes of individual doctors, and you still may have to pay. Those same groups who oppose abortion are also involved in campaigns to restrict health information and sex education, and refuse to accept that fear and ignorance will not only increase the number of abortions, but will threaten the lives and health of thousands of women.

Most abortions are done early in pregnancy – before 12 weeks. Changes to the abortion law which would restrict these abortions have so far been unsuccessful, and anti-abortionists now concentrate on stopping later abortions. Once again they are unable to accept that an improvement in health education, contraception and early abortion facilities would in fact achieve this aim. Research into those who have late abortions shows clearly that many have actually sought help *before* they were 12 weeks pregnant, but the operations have been delayed by doctors and administrators. Others may not know they are pregnant for many weeks, or be paralysed by fear of telling anyone that they are. A late abortion in any circumstances is much more likely to be emotionally traumatic as well as posing a greater risk to health and subsequent fertility, but the need for it won't disappear simply by making it illegal.

The decision to have an abortion, even if it is to be done early in pregnancy, is likely to involve many complex issues. It means thinking about your life both now and in the future, and having to be prepared to take on what may be far-reaching consequences of your actions. It can never be a casual decision, made without emotion and then forgotten. However sure you may be that it is the right thing to do, you may still have some feelings of conflict about your decision, and you will almost certainly remember it and the circumstances in which it was made for the rest of your life. Anti-abortionists insult women with the suggestion that the decision to have an abortion is made casually or carelessly, and demean us with the equation that to have mixed feelings is the same as being irresponsible or confused.

Confirming the pregnancy

The experience of very early pregnancy varies from woman to woman. Sometimes it is hard to distinguish from the pre-menstrual phase. You might have tender and swollen breasts, or feel more tired than usual. You might also feel a bit sick, though this is more likely later in pregnancy and not in the first week or two. A very frequent sign of very early pregnancy is wanting to pee more often.

The most common and reliable sign of pregnancy is a missed period, but you don't have to wait that long for confirmation. It's now possible to have a blood test to confirm pregnancy within ten days of conception. You have to wait 24 hours for the results, so you ring or go back to the clinic the day after you have the test. This is available from pregnancy advisory services and some family planning clinics and GPs.

There is a range of urine tests available which can also tell you whether or not you are pregnant. Earlier versions can only do this once your period is two weeks late, but there are now tests available which can check for pregnancy on the day that your period is due, or two or three days later. You can buy these tests at your chemist. Some packs contain two testing kits, so if the first test is negative you can test yourself again a week later if you still have not had a period.

You work out how many weeks pregnant you are by counting the weeks from the first day of your last period. Even though you probably ovulated and conceived about a fortnight after this time doctors always base their assessments of the pregnancy on the last period date. So if the first day of the last period was six weeks ago, you will be described as six weeks pregnant.

If you go to a pregnancy advisory service and to some GPs and family planning clinics and chemists, you can get the results of the test immediately. Your period needs to be 14 days late for this kind of test. You may prefer to have a test at a clinic or advisory service, because it means you won't be on your own when you get the result, and you'll have the chance to talk about what has happened as soon as you know. Check beforehand whether you'll get the results there and then – you can end up waiting a week or so for the results of an NHS test.

The cost of the test depends where you have it done. Urine tests bought over the counter at the chemist cost around £6, as does a blood test at a pregnancy advisory service. Urine tests at a pregnancy advisory service will cost about £3. You can get the result of these tests within 24 hours, and sometimes on the same day. An NHS test will be free, but you may have to wait several days for the result.

You should have a test if you have any reason to believe you might be pregnant. It is possible, even though you are pregnant, to have a light period-like bleed at the time your period is due.

A doctor can also confirm pregnancy by doing an internal examination. If there is any doubt about the duration of the pregnancy, or there are suspicions that it might be ectopic (outside the uterus), you can have an ultrasound scan.

Making the decision

How and why women decide to have abortions varies enormously. You may have split up with the man with whom you got pregnant, or just started the relationship, or had intercourse with him only once and never saw him again. You might have already had your desired number of children, and be unable, for reasons both practical and emotional, to have another. You may be in a good and stable relationship, but feel that now is not the right time to have a child. There are probably as many reasons for abortion as there are women who have one.

Even if you were clear you didn't want to be pregnant at the moment, your feelings once you know that you are may surprise you. If you've never been pregnant before, having this confirmation that you are fertile, and that you could have a child, may be very exciting. But equally the prospect of continuing this unplanned pregnancy, and the way in which it would completely change your life, may be terrifying and mean that there is no question of going on with it. You may simply not be in a position to care for a child — emotionally or materially.

The discussions you have about your situation and what the options are will be very important at this time. As well as discussing it with your sexual partner it may be very helpful to talk with close friends and relations. It is very likely that someone you know has had a similar experience, and will be able to offer practical advice (perhaps about local clinics and doctors) as well as first-hand understanding about how you are feeling now.

If you are in a steady relationship with the man with whom you've got pregnant, you may want to make a joint decision about whether or not to continue the pregnancy. You may both be sure that abortion is the best alternative, with both of you prepared to take responsibility for the decision. He can continue to provide support throughout the next few weeks — he can come with you to the doctor or clinic, and then be there and take more domestic responsibility when you've had the operation and need time to recuperate. He can pay half or all the cost of the operation if you have to go privately. But even though there may not be any conflict between you about whether or not you have this operation, it can still put a lot of stress on the relationship. You may feel resentful that it's you who has to go through the experience of the pregnancy and abortion, and he may feel powerless and irrelevant in relation to what is happening.

There may be disagreement between you about whether or not to have an abortion. Discovering that your partner has assumed you will have an abortion when you have not yet made up your mind can be very upsetting. It's difficult not to feel pressured into the decision to terminate the pregnancy, even though you might know deep down that it is a step you would have wanted to take in the end anyway. You need to find out from him what support he is prepared to give if you *do* continue the pregnancy, and consider what effect this would have on your relationship with him, and yours and his with the child. Would you be able to manage on your own if you had to? Involvement, discussion and support from friends and relations who haven't got such a direct vested interest in your decision may be particularly important now. If the situation is reversed, and he wants the pregnancy to continue and you don't, you are also likely to feel under considerable pressure. You may know that you could be risking the relationship by having an abortion, but feel that you don't have any choice because you also know that continuing this pregnancy is out of the question.

Sometimes it's difficult to know exactly what your partner feels about the pregnancy, and whether or not he wants you to go on with it. He may say 'it's up to you' and that he'll support whatever decision you make. Whilst superficially it may seem more acceptable that he is deferring to a woman's right to choose, rather than expressing a definite preference either way, in practice it is often less than helpful. Can he *really* have no strong feelings about his own possible future as a father and being in a long-term relationship with you? Or is he assuming that you will decide to have an abortion, and doesn't want to be involved in the decision? For many men this equivocal position seems to be a way of absolving themselves of responsibility for what will happen. If you do decide to continue the pregnancy there may be no way of knowing when or if he is suddenly going to tell you he never wanted a child anyway, and that you forced him into it. You need to know what he feels now, and to have some idea of what this means for the future.

It could be that you decide never to tell the man with whom you got pregnant, because you don't have any genuine involvement with him apart from what may be only one single experience of sex. You have to decide for yourself whether you need any further involvement from him, and what difference it will make both to your decision and the way you feel about making it. Would you have had any contact with him if it weren't for this pregnancy and, if you are sure you want to have an abortion, what help will he be if he knows? These are very difficult questions and you are the only person who can answer them. Some would say that the man should be told, and should take continuing responsibility for what he was at least 50 per cent responsible for in the first place. But such calling to account can be needlessly and additionally upsetting when you've already decided that you are going to have an abortion, even though making this decision on your own can make you feel isolated and miserable. Try to involve a close friend or relation who can help you through and provide the continuing support that you might need afterwards.

An unplanned pregnancy often seems to happen as part of a series of apparently unrelated problems. You may have just lost your job, had difficulties in your relationship, or be in the middle of a financial crisis. It's at times like these that you can lose control over other parts of your life – in this case, contraception. Because you're preoccupied by other things you can forget to take your pill, or lose track of which part of the menstrual cycle you're in. Stress itself can have an effect on the menstrual cycle, making you ovulate earlier or later than usual. So on top of everything else you then find yourself pregnant, and having to make a difficult decision at a time when you feel least up to making it.

Counselling

Everyone who is considering an abortion should have the opportunity for some kind of counselling, in which they can discuss all the alternatives and explore their feelings about the pregnancy and its implications. In the NHS this counselling may be provided by a doctor – either your GP or a hospital doctor – as well as by a social worker, nurse or pregnancy counsellor. You may feel that counselling is unnecessary in your case – you've decided that you need to have an abortion, and the explanation and discussion of the reasons with an outsider whom you don't know isn't much more than a formality. But you could equally well feel that counselling is important, and in this case it's vital you should have it.

If you feel you are not getting the opportunity for discussion that you need (which can sometimes happen in the NHS where doctors sometimes concentrate on the practical and medical aspects of abortion, and not on your feelings about it), you can always see a counsellor at a pregnancy advisory service. It doesn't matter if you are already booked in with the NHS – you don't have to have a private operation because you've had private counselling. If you go to a pregnancy advisory service in the private sector you will always see a counsellor before seeing a doctor. The helpfulness of counselling will depend on the experience and expertise of the person you see. The counsellor should not tell you what to do, but listen to what you're saying and enable you to get clear about what you want, so that there is a minimum of risk that you will regret the decision later. She should also be able to give you information about alternatives to abortion, including adoption and fostering, as well as other practical details about maternity benefits and support.

You should also have an opportunity to discuss future contraception at this stage (see page 197). You may want to change methods, or to start using contraception if you haven't been using it before. The counsellor or doctor should also tell you what will happen during the operation, discuss with you what kind of anaesthetic you will have (see page 192) and give you information about how to look after yourself afterwards.

Ambivalence – when you're not sure

It's always difficult to be 100 per cent sure that your decision about the pregnancy is the right one. Even if it is overwhelmingly clear that you cannot continue the pregnancy, you may also feel very strong urges to go on with it. You may have not wanted to get pregnant, but now that you are you feel almost fatalistic about it – it's happened, so it might as well continue. And supposing this is your only chance, supposing that you never get pregnant again and are denying yourself this one opportunity to have a child? However much you know about the safety of abortion, and that it won't affect subsequent fertility, you may still worry that your fertility will be put at risk.

Good counselling should enable you to disentangle all these conflicting feelings, as well as giving you the chance to look as objectively as you can at your practical circumstances. What would it mean to have a baby now? What kind of life do you envisage for the baby in the future, as well as for you and your partner if you have one?

It is vital that you give yourself enough time to think through and discuss all the options, and don't rush into a decision either way. Many women fear that the longer they are pregnant the more ambivalent they will become, and instead of acknowledging this ambivalence try to speed up the whole process: because you are worried that you won't want an abortion next week, it has to be done tomorrow. You have to remember that even if the abortion is done quickly, you will have a lot of time – maybe years – to think about it, and you need to be able to look back and feel that you considered all the alternatives when you decided to have the abortion.

Whilst of course there is a limit to the time you can spend thinking about the decision, a week or so in early pregnancy will not make any difference to the safety of the operation. You could see a counsellor and then wait for a while before seeing a doctor, or give yourself a week before seeing anyone about a possible termination. You could see the counsellor more than once if you wish. A doctor is unlikely to agree to an abortion if she believes you to be ambivalent, but many will let you have the time in which to come to a considered decision if you need it.

The abortion law and its interpretations

Two doctors have to agree to you having an abortion, and both have to sign a form saying they have agreed. You should be seen and examined by both doctors. The first doctor could be your GP, who can sign the form and then refer you to a consultant at the local hospital. You will see two doctors (as well as a counsellor) at a pregnancy advisory service.

The interpretation of the 1967 Abortion Act depends very much on the personal attitudes of individual doctors. Some doctors do not believe in abortion unless continuing the pregnancy would put your health seriously at risk, and some have moral objections to abortion in almost any circumstances. If the doctor is personally opposed to abortion she should refer you to another doctor who doesn't have this attitude. You are free to go to another doctor even if the first doctor doesn't make this referral – either an NHS doctor or one at a pregnancy advisory service.

The 1967 Abortion Act has four clauses, and your reasons for the abortion can come under one or more of them.

1 The continuance of the pregnancy would involve risk to your life greater than if the pregnancy were terminated. There is very wide interpretation of this clause. Since it is actually safer to have an abortion before 12 weeks than it is to continue a pregnancy, some doctors would say that any woman who is less than 12 weeks pregnant can have an abortion under this clause. Others would want proof of some kind of severe illness or physical problem that would mean it is especially dangerous for you to continue the pregnancy.

2 The continuance of the pregnancy would involve risk of injury to your physical or mental health greater than if the pregnancy were terminated. The most important part of this clause is 'mental health'. If continuing the pregnancy presents a considerable risk of depression and anxiety – as it could do if the pregnancy is unplanned and unwanted – then you can qualify for an abortion under this clause. The majority of abortions are done under this clause.

3 The continuance of the pregnancy would involve risk of injury to the physical or mental health of your existing children greater than if the pregnancy were terminated. If you already have children, and they would suffer in some way by your having another, you are eligible for an abortion.

4 There is substantial risk that if the child were born it would suffer from such physical or mental abnormality as to be seriously handicapped. You could have an abortion under this clause if screening during pregnancy had shown that the foetus suffers from some kind of abnormality, like spina bifida, Down's

Syndrome, or some other hereditary disease. It would also be possible if you've had rubella (German measles) during early pregnancy, which can also result in foetal abnormality.

It is possible to have an abortion within the first 24 weeks of pregnancy. This limit has been set by the Department of Health after a review of the definition of foetal viability (the ability of the foetus to survive outside a woman's body). In practice this means few doctors will operate beyond 22 weeks because it can be difficult to diagnose the exact duration of pregnancy.

NHS or private?

The private sector, which includes non-profit-making pregnancy advisory services, does more than half of all abortions in England and Wales. The availability of NHS abortion facilities varies widely around the country, with some health authorities providing prompt and good day-care services, and others allowing hospital consultants to enact their own personal objections to NHS abortion so that few are done in particular districts.

The abortion law is the same whether you have the operation done privately or on the NHS. It's the interpretation of the law that may differ, and how much your own feelings about the pregnancy will be taken into account. Though many doctors in the NHS are sympathetic and helpful, doctors who work as part of a pregnancy advisory service are more likely to base their interpretation of the law on what you tell them, and how you describe your present and forseeable circumstances.

Doctors working in the private sector are also more likely to be prepared to do later abortions, and when they do, to use dilation and evacuation (D and E) rather than prostaglandin induction (see page 197). Abortion statistics show that in 1984 32 per cent of NHS abortions over 12 weeks were performed using dilation and evacuation, with 57 per cent terminated using prostaglandin. In the private sector the figures were 60 per cent and 35 per cent respectively. (The remaining percentage were done with other methods.) It requires greater skill to perform a late D & E, which may be one reason why the private sector does more operations in this way. But prostaglandin induction is frequently more traumatic for the woman (see page 199), so you may prefer to go privately if you want to avoid this.

You should first see your GP, who can refer you for an NHS abortion. The GP can do a pregnancy test, and may want to examine you. Most GPs are sympathetic about abortion, and should refer you on if they can. But if the GP knows that the local consultant is hostile to abortion, she may suggest you go to a pregnancy advisory service, and may provide you with a referral letter that you can take with you (though this is not necessary, and the advisory service will see you with or without a letter from your doctor).

Even if it is possible to have an abortion on the NHS in your area, you could find that you have to wait, both for a consultation with a doctor at the hospital and for the operation itself. Your GP should know the routine at the local hospital, consultants' attitudes, and how long you might have to wait, as should the family planning clinic. A local women's group or centre may be able to tell you about facilities nearby, and whether any delays are likely. They may also do pregnancy tests. The Community Health Council may also have some idea of waiting lists and of hospital doctors' attitudes to abortion.

You don't have to tell your GP about the pregnancy, or that you want an abortion, if you don't want to. You can go straight to a pregnancy advisory service without a referral, and the doctor won't be told unless you agree to this. But if your GP doesn't know it will almost certainly mean that you won't be able to have a day-care abortion, so you'll have to stay at the clinic overnight. Do tell your GP if you possibly can, so that if the (unlikely) need arises you can get treatment for any problems after the operation. It may be important in the future for the doctor to know that you've been pregnant, especially if it is this doctor who provides you with contraception. Remember that all consultations with your doctor are confidential. She should not give information about you to anyone else.

Pregnancy advisory services should be able to see you within a few days, and be able to arrange the operation within a week or so. You are also more likely to get good and informed counselling at pregnancy advisory services, though once again this is often available within the NHS.

The major disadvantage of going privately is that you'll have to pay. Fees at the time of writing are around £20 for consultation with the counsellor and doctors, and £140 for the operation if it's done before 12 weeks. After 12 weeks the operation will cost £200. In cases of extreme financial hardship the advisory service may be able to help with a loan, or even to arrange for you to go to the NHS.

Having an abortion – what happens

You will be seen and examined by two doctors before you have the operation. These doctors could be your GP and a consultant at a local hospital, or a doctor and consultant at a pregnancy advisory service. The doctors will examine you internally to confirm that you are pregnant, and also to check how many weeks pregnant you are. A manual examination of this kind can confirm the duration of the pregnancy to within one or two weeks.

You will be asked a series of questions about your medical history. The doctor will need to know whether or not you have been pregnant before and what happened, so you'll need to tell her about any previous abortions, miscarriages or births. You will also be asked about any major operations you have had in the recent past, and whether you have any history of thrombosis or other blood problems. You should tell the doctor if you have any long-term physical problem like epilepsy, or are on any drug treatment at the moment.

The doctor or nurse will take your blood pressure, and you will also have a blood and urine test. This is to check whether you have any health problems you don't already know about, like anaemia or diabetes. Your blood group is also checked. If you are found to be Rhesus negative, and this is your first pregnancy, you will have to be given a drug called *anti-D immunoglobulin* after the operation to stop your body building up anti-bodies that could affect future pregnancies.

If you are going to start a new method of contraception at the same time as the abortion (see page 197) the doctor should check that it is safe for you to use the particular method in the usual way – family history of cardiovascular problems for the pill, history of PID or ectopic pregnancy for the IUD, etc.

Abortion before 12 weeks – vacuum aspiration

Nearly all abortions done before 12 weeks use the vacuum aspiration (suction) method. A flexible tube (vacurette) is inserted through the cervix, connected to a suction pump, and the contents of the uterus sucked out.

Vacuum aspiration is a quick operation. It usually takes about ten minutes from start to finish.

The anaesthetic – general or local?

If you have an abortion before 12 weeks you may be offered a choice between a general (when you are asleep) or local (when you are awake) anaesthetic. Most early abortions in this country are done under general anaesthetic, though in many other countries the reverse is true – in the US, for example, an estimated 80 per cent of abortions under 12 weeks are done under local anaesthetic.

General anaesthetic always carries a slight risk if you have blood pressure problems or other cardiovascular conditions. And even though the general anaesthetic used is a light one, and you will lose consciousness for only 30 minutes or so, it can still take some time to recover afterwards. You may feel or be sick, and be sleepy or muzzy for an hour or so once you're awake. The advantage is that you won't know anything about the operation.

A local anaesthetic means you will be conscious throughout the operation, and you won't have to recover from the effects of the general anaesthetic. The doctor will inject the local into your cervix, and you should not have any pain while the cervix is being dilated. There might be some cramps and dragging pains whilst the vacuum aspiration is being done (see page 194), but the more relaxed you are, the less these will be. If you think it is likely that you will be very tense and anxious with a local anaesthetic it may be best to have a general. It may be possible to have a counsellor, or even a friend or relation with you while you have the operation. If the clinic or hospital does not permit this the doctor and nurse should be able to talk you through the operation and provide any reassurance that you need.

Preparing for the operation

The hospital or clinic should tell you their preferred routine. You may go in the day before the operation, or you may be asked to arrive an hour or so before the operation. You should take some sanitary towels with you to use after the operation, when you might have some bleeding (see page 196). You should not use tampons because these can increase the risk of infection.

You should not eat or drink for eight hours before the operation, so as to reduce the chance of nausea or vomiting after a general anaesthetic. Some hospitals will give you an *enema* which makes you empty your bowels before the operation, but this is increasingly less common. You do not need to have your pubic hair shaved off before the operation, though some hospitals still do this.

You should take off any jewellery, and remove false teeth and contact lenses before the operation.

If you are having a general anaesthetic you may be given a *pre-med* which makes you feel a bit sleepy before the general is given. The general anaesthetic might be given before you are taken into the operating theatre, or be given in the theatre itself.

You won't need a pre-med if you are having a local anaesthetic, though it is possible to have a tranquilliser beforehand. You can walk into the operating theatre, and lie on the couch. You then open your legs wide apart and put your feet in stirrups or rest your knees on pads so that your body stays still.

The operation

The vagina and cervix must be clean before the operation begins, so they are wiped with antiseptic. The doctor will then insert a speculum into your vagina to bring the cervix fully into view and to separate the vaginal walls. The doctor then puts in a *tentaculum* which holds the cervix still. If you are having a local anaesthetic it will then be put into your cervix with a series of injections that feel a bit like little bee-stings as the needle enters the cervical tissue. The doctor will wait until the anaesthetic has taken effect before proceeding with the opening (dilation) of the cervix and the operation, so you may have to wait for a minute or so.

The cervix has first to be dilated so that the curette can be inserted into the uterus. This is done with a series of metal instruments called *dilators* which are inserted into the cervical opening until the cervix has opened the required amount. The degree of dilation depends on how many weeks pregnant you are. The greater the number of weeks, the greater the dilation. For a ten-week pregnancy your cervix will probably be dilated 8mm. Dilation can also be done by giving you an injection or vaginal pessary of the hormone prostaglandin a few hours before the operation, or by inserting a *laminaria tent* into your cervix the day before. This is a little cylinder that swells when it gets moist, gradually dilating the cervix as it does so.

Once the cervix has been dilated to the required extent, the dilator is removed and the flexible plastic vacurette is inserted. It is then connected to the suction machine, the *aspirator*. The doctor will move the vacurette around the internal surface of your uterus, with all the contents (foetus, placenta and amniotic sac and fluid) being sucked out as she does so. The doctor can check the contents of your uterus once they have been removed so as to make sure that there are no bits of tissue left inside the uterus.

If you have a local anaesthetic you may have cramps like bad period pains during the operation and immediately afterwards. These cramps may be worse if you haven't had children and your cervix is tight. If you have a general anaesthetic you may wake up with these cramps after the operation when the anaesthetic has worn off. The cramps happen as your uterus goes back to its usual non-pregnant size.

In the days after the abortion all the symptoms of pregnancy will gradually disappear. Your breasts will go back to their normal size. If you have had nausea during the pregnancy it should stop immediately.

Physical complications during and after early abortion

Complications of early abortion are now rare, because techniques have improved considerably over the years. Some can happen during the operation itself, in which case the doctor will know and be able to take action immediately. Others only show themselves in the days after the operation, and you should return either to your GP or to a doctor at the pregnancy advisory service if you are worried about anything.

● **Perforation of the uterus** can happen during dilation of the cervix or be caused by the curette tearing the uterine wall. Heavy bleeding can follow. If the perforation is severe the doctor may have to do a laparoscopy (see page 170) in order to complete the abortion. A severe perforation will have to be mended by the doctor, but a small perforation will probably heal on its own. In either case you will almost certainly have to stay at the hospital or clinic until bleeding is normal and you are quite well.

● **Very heavy bleeding** immediately after the operation could be caused by damage to the cervix or uterus, or by uterine perforation. The doctor should sew up any tears in the cervix. Further investigation (maybe with laparoscopy) will be needed if the heavy bleeding does not stop and uterine damage is suspected. In *very rare cases* it may be necessary for the uterus to be removed (hysterectomy) if nothing else can be done to stop the bleeding, and it is continued and severe (haemorrhage).

Heavy bleeding starting a few days after the operation could mean the abortion is incomplete, and that small pieces of placenta are still in the uterus. This could also be accompanied by vaginal discharge and continuing uterine cramps, so return to your doctor if any of these happen. The doctor can prescribe a drug to stop this bleeding, but if it continues you may have to have what amounts to another abortion to remove the retained tissue.

● **Failed abortion**, when the pregnancy continues after the operation, is very rare indeed. The doctor should know whether or not the operation was successful by checking the contents of the uterus after the abortion. If there was no uterine pregnancy, but the symptoms of pregnancy continue, you could have an ectopic pregnancy (see page 164). This needs immediate treatment.

● **Infection** can be avoided if you follow all the rules about looking after yourself in the days after the abortion (see below). If you don't, and use tampons instead of sanitary towels, or have intercourse soon after the operation, bacteria could enter the vagina and infect the uterus. It can also happen if you had an infection *before* the operation, making you vulnerable to additional risk of infection after the operation. In rare cases infection can occur because of bacteria entering the vagina and uterus during the operation itself – if the surgical instruments were not sterile, for instance.

Symptoms of pelvic infection can include abnormal bleeding, a heavy or bad smelling vaginal discharge, pain in the lower abdomen, nausea, and raised temperature. It's important to act quickly if you think you may have an infection, as it can be treated right away with antibiotics. If the infection goes on untreated you could become seriously ill, and it could damage your reproductive organs so that your future fertility is affected.

Looking after yourself following an abortion

You will probably want to rest for a day or so after the abortion. You may still have cramps a bit like period pains, and you may also have some bleeding like a light period. This may go on for a few days, and may get slightly heavier a couple of days after the operation, and then subside.

You should not put anything inside your vagina for three weeks after the operation. This means you should not use tampons, have sexual intercourse, or douche (wash your vagina) during this time. These safety measures will minimise the risk of infection.

You should see a doctor within two to four weeks after the operation, but go back before that if you have any worries about your recovery. This check-up should involve an internal examination to check that the abortion was completed properly and you're not still pregnant.

Contraception after early abortion

You can go on the pill the same day as you have the abortion. You won't be able to rely on it until after 14 days of taking it. Since you should not be having intercourse during this time there will be no need for any additional contraceptive.

An IUD can be inserted at the same time as the abortion. There is no reported increase in the rate of IUD expulsion or of any other IUD complication if it is inserted at this time. This avoids having to go through the experience of IUD insertion (see page 159) at a later date, but will mean that you are likely to have additional cramps caused by the insertion of the IUD as well as the abortion.

You can leave sorting out future contraception until you return for your check-up after the abortion if you prefer.

Your future fertility

There is no evidence that a single abortion before 12 weeks has any effect on future fertility, unless you have a severe infection afterwards. Because abortion techniques have improved so much this is now very rare. It has been suggested that more than one abortion could mean that your cervix gets weakened, and miscarriage is more likely, but there is little research evidence as yet to back this supposition. Neither is it clear as yet whether later abortion (over 12 weeks) will make any difference to your later fertility, but research is under way into this.

Abortion after 12 weeks

Two methods are used to perform abortions over 12 weeks: dilation and evacuation (D and E) and prostaglandin induction. Pregnancies of between 12 and 16 weeks are almost always terminated using D and E, and both D and E and prostaglandin induction are used over 16 weeks. The former appears to be more commonly used than prostaglandin in the private sector, but it is not known why.

Dilation and evacuation involves preliminaries similar to those for a vacuum aspiration, but because the pregnancy is over 12 weeks your cervix will have to be dilated more. The doctor then removes the pregnancy using forceps, a curette, and vacuum aspiration. This operation takes longer than an earlier vacuum aspiration, and is always done under general anaesthetic. The anaesthetic will last longer than for an earlier abortion, so the after-effects (nausea and muzziness) might be greater and last longer. You will definitely have to stay overnight at the clinic or hospital.

Prostaglandin is a chemical which induces a miscarriage. Saline (salt solution) or urea are also used sometimes, but rarely in this country nowadays. Prostaglandin is preferable because it carries fewer risks and is quicker. You will be awake throughout the procedure, but should be offered tranquillisers and drugs to reduce pain.

Prostaglandin is injected into the uterus, just outside the amniotic sac. This can be done either by injecting through the abdominal wall below your navel (after a local anaesthetic to numb the part of the abdomen through which the needle will go) or by injecting through the cervical entrance to the uterus. This procedure is repeated every 4-6 hours until the pregnancy starts to miscarry, and may be combined with the injection of another miscarriage-inducing chemical, oxytocin. Prostaglandin can also be given in the form of a vaginal pessary or an intra-venous (into a vein) drip.

You then will have to wait for the miscarriage to start. This takes an average of 12-16 hours, but can take longer – more than 24 hours in some cases. The miscarriage will then begin, starting with the breaking of the amniotic sac and the loss of amniotic fluid from the uterus into the vagina, and quickly followed by mild uterine contractions which gradually increase and become more painful. Even though the pregnancy is not as big as it would be at full-term, the labour you experience may be very painful. It may take some hours of contractions before you expel the amniotic fluid, foetus and placenta.

There is a chance, if the pregnancy is over 20 weeks and prostaglandin is used, that the foetus could be born alive, but it is unlikely to be able to live for more than a few minutes.

There should be someone with you throughout the time you have a prostaglandin induction, and you should be able to have all the tranquillisers and pain controlling drugs that you need as well as continued reassurance. It is bound to be a difficult and upsetting experience, and you will need to do what you can to prepare yourself emotionally before it happens. Learning the breathing techniques used in full-term labour can help you through the pain of the contractions.

Prostaglandin induction may be followed by dilation and curettage of your uterus to make sure that the operation has worked and no tissue is left in your uterus. You will have to stay at the clinic or hospital for at least a night afterwards.

You will need constant medical monitoring throughout the procedure, so that any complications can be dealt with. Haemorrhage (heavy and uncontrollable bleeding) is more likely with late abortion than with vacuum aspiration. After the abortion you should follow the routine for looking after yourself described on page 196. You may want to rest for several days afterwards, as the experience has probably been very tiring.

Opinions differ about which of the two methods is better for your health and subsequent fertility. Some doctors believe that D and E is more likely to result in a weakened cervix, and increased chance of miscarriage in a later (wanted) pregnancy. Others think an abortion under general anaesthetic is less traumatic and so preferable.

After an abortion – if there's guilt or regret

Regret and depression can follow an abortion done early or late in pregnancy. Just as it is difficult to be 100 per cent sure that an abortion is the right thing to decide, it can be hard to look back and feel 100 per cent sure that it was the right thing to have had done.

While many women feel enormous relief after an abortion, this can be mixed with considerable sadness that it had to happen at all. You may feel absolutely sure that you couldn't have done anything else in the circumstances, but still feel miserable and upset about it. You could also feel angry – with your partner, with yourself, with friends who don't seem to appreciate how distressing the experience has been, and with the whole business of sex and contraception that precipitated this situation.

It can be particularly difficult if having an abortion conflicts with your moral or religious beliefs. You may feel very guilty about what you have done, and that it's gone against your basic principles – this can happen even if you were sure that you could not continue the pregnancy. You may feel guilty about having got pregnant, especially if you feel that you did so because you didn't use contraception properly. You can even feel guilty because you *don't* feel depressed, and be worried that you are selfish and uncaring because you feel happy and relieved once the abortion is over.

Research shows that serious depression after abortion is rare, and that the risk of it can be minimised by good counselling and thorough discussion of your feelings beforehand. But it has also been recognised that women often need follow-up counselling and an opportunity to discuss their feelings after an abortion. You can always return to a pregnancy advisory service, perhaps to the counsellor you originally saw, to talk about it some more. You also might be able to get in touch with a post-abortion support group, where you can talk with other women who are going through similar experiences. A local women's centre or information service may have details of such groups. The marriage guidance council, or any other local counselling service could also offer support. Books written by women about the abortion experience may also help (see page 206). What's important is that you find some way of exploring and resolving your feelings about what has happened.

13

FERTILITY CONTROL
The Future

There are no signs of any genuinely new contraceptive method arriving on the market in the immediate future. Most of the new methods are likely to be for women, carrying on the twentieth-century tradition of female responsibility for birth control. The new products that we *can* expect are mostly variations on the methods that already exist, and research into other ways of preventing conception continues.

But future versions of contraceptives such as the pill and IUD may still stand as advances in contraceptive technology, since they could well pose fewer health risks and be more effective. The information below is likely to change as more research is done, but should give you some idea of the kinds of contraceptive that are likely to be available in years to come.

Barrier methods

The 'Contracap' would be used without a spermicide and worn continuously for several months. It has a one-way valve which enables the passage of cervical mucus and menstrual blood, but prevents the entry of sperm into the uterus. But the current design may have to be modified, since it may not be sufficiently effective as a contraceptive.

Diaphragms, vaginal rings and other devices impregnated with spermicide would mean there was no need to use additional cream or jelly, so the device would be easier to insert. Results of research trials are not yet known.

New sorts of spermicides may be developed which don't need to be used with a barrier. A drug previously used in treating heart disease, Proprandol, could be made into a vaginal spermicide. It is thought to be very effective but trials continue. Other new spermicides include a substance called RS 37367, and compounds of the chemical benzalkonium. Either of these could be used in the new spermicide-releasing barrier methods.

Drugs that thicken cervical mucus could also be introduced. Instead of using a device like the cap or diaphragm the drug would make your body produce its own cervical barrier to sperm. Ovulation and the menstrual cycle would not be affected.

What is in fact a barrier method, but in some ways is more like a reversible method of sterilisation, are removable plugs placed in the fallopian tubes which would prevent the meeting of egg and sperm. These would have to be fitted and removed by a doctor.

Fertility awareness

One of the main problems in using fertility awareness methods is finding a way to detect ovulation accurately. Whilst the symptothermal method can be very reliable indeed, it may still be difficult to predict ovulation, especially in an irregular menstrual cycle, so it may be necessary to avoid intercourse for a number of days. One way of being more sure about which are the fertile times is by using a special dipstick that can detect the chemical changes in urine or saliva that happen at ovulation. This aid to fertility awareness is not yet generally available, but it is possible to obtain the 'Bioself 110' — a thermometer which uses a microchip to calculate when you are fertile. The device has first to be programmed with details of your temperature changes during the menstrual cycle. There seems no reason to think that this is going to be any more reliable than taking your temperature yourself and recording it on a chart, but it could save time. More reliable would be detection of ovulation using an ultrasound scan, but it seems unlikely that this method could be developed and marketed so that women could do the scans themselves.

Hormonal methods

Most of the hormonal methods·currently being researched involve new ways of delivering the oestrogen and progestogen into the body (the same two hormones that are in the pill). Nasal sprays, hormone-impregnated bracelets, cervical devices, vaginal rings and once-a-month pills are all being researched. Smaller amounts of hormone are likely to be needed using these methods of delivery, with (it is to be hoped) an accompanying decrease in other effects on the body.

There is also research into the use of other hormones to prevent pregnancy. These are likely to be synthetic versions of the natural hormones that are produced during the menstrual cycle.

New designs of IUD

There has been research into threadless IUDs in the hope that the lack of a thread would reduce the risk of pelvic infection. But though this aspect of IUD-related problems could be reduced, there may be others that are increased. It would be impossible to check that the IUD is still in place, as it is at the moment by feeling for the strings. One solution for this problem is an IUD that contains a magnet. A doctor could then tell whether the IUD was in place by passing a compass over your lower abdomen. Whether family planning clinics would be willing to issue IUD-users with this kind of orienteering kit remains to be seen.

The Progestasert is an IUD impregnated with progestogen. It can be left inside your body for only a year, and is not available on the NHS in this country. The rate of ectopic pregnancies is higher than with other IUDs. New hormone-releasing IUDs are also being developed, and one has been described as being suitable for up to nine years' use.

A pill for men

Though it's a story which hits the headlines about once a year, there is as yet no sign of a pill for men which is likely to be used on the same scale as the pill for women. Whereas it is relatively easy to stop the production of a single monthly egg, there seems to be considerable difficulty in stopping the constant production of sperm. Hormonal preparations often seem to cause loss of libido, and so cannot be used. Researchers, it seems, have no problem in believing the men who experience this, though they've often had difficulty in believing women on the contraceptive pill who have similar problems. A hormonal cream rubbed on the belly was successful in stopping sperm production in men, but had masculinising effects on their female partners who came into contact with the cream when they were making love.

Gossypol, a chemical derived from cottonseed oil, has been found to be very effective in stopping the movement of sperm, but fertility appears to take some considerable time to return. There is a possibility it could cause other health problems too, but research trials continue. A number of other chemicals (some used as part of drug treatments for disorders that have nothing to do with the reproductive system) have also been found to affect sperm. Some of these chemicals may be used to create new spermicides to be used by women, rather than a male pill.

A chemical called *inhibin* may prove able to be used by men and women to stop both ovulation and sperm production. There have recently been reports that this can be done without causing other effects on the body, but once again the development and marketing of such a product is a long way off.

Contraceptive vaccine

It could become possible to immunise a woman against her partner's sperm and to immunise men against their own sperm. This means that sperm-rejecting antibodies would be produced, making conception impossible. No one has discovered a way of doing this as yet, and certainly not a way which could be reversed at a later date. But research has come up with a vaccine that makes a woman's body reject a fertilised egg. The vaccine works by stopping production of the pregnancy hormone HCG (see page 114) which maintains a pregnancy once fertilisation has taken place. It would therefore result in a very early abortion, and so there may be political objections to such a method being introduced.

Reversible sterilisation

There is as yet no way of doing a sterilisation operation that is definitely reversible, although some surgeons find that certain sorts of sterilisation operations are easier to reverse than others. Use of an easily removable clip, tap or plug in both men and women, with the minimum of damage to either the fallopian tubes or the vas deferens could well be a popular way of stopping conception for those who want a long-term but not permanent method of contraception.

The abortion pill

RU 486 is the name of a drug which can produce an abortion up to eight weeks after conception. It starts menstruation and destroys the embryo if you are pregnant. The drug is an anti-progesterone, which counteracts the progesterone which makes the lining of the uterus ready for implantation and also maintains the pregnancy. RU 486 could be used before pregnancy is confirmed, as well as after. It is not yet clear how reliable the method would be, or what other effects on the body it might have. The idea of the drug's developers is that instead of using contraception women could use RU 486 regularly (once every menstrual cycle) to avoid pregnancy. Anti-abortionists are already opposed to the drug, and also to the spectre of women being able to perform a safe 'home abortion' without medical supervision or consent. They also say that introduction of the drug would result in 'a black market supplying the drug to women who would take it home and not use it properly'. Manufacturers say RU 486 could be generally available within the next few years, but a political battle is likely before it is available for us to use it as and when we choose.

FURTHER READING

Contraception – Your Questions Answered, John Guillebaud, Pitman, 1985

Coping with Abortion, Alison Frater and Catherine Wright, Chambers, 1986

The Fight for Family Planning, Audrey Leathard, Macmillan, 1980

The IUD – A Woman's Guide, Robert Snowden, Unwin Paperbacks, 1986

Handbook of Family Planning, editor Nancy Loudon, Churchill Livingstone, 1985

Marie Stopes – A Biography, Ruth Hall, Andre Deutsch, 1978

The Manual of Natural Family Planning, Anna Flynn and Melissa Brooks, Unwin Paperbacks, 1985

Natural Birth Control: A Practical Guide to Fertility Awareness, Katia and Jonathan Drake, Thorsons, 1984

Our Bodies Ourselves, Angela Phillips and Jill Rakusen, Penguin Books, 1978, revised ed. to appear in 1988

The Pill, John Guillebaud, Oxford University Press, 1984

Sex and Destiny, Germaine Greer, Penguin, 1984

The Sexual Politics of Reproduction, editor Hilary Homans, Gower, 1985

Understanding Abortion, Mary Pipes, Women's Press, 1985

Whose Choice – What Women Have to Say About Contraception, Oxford women's health action group, 1984

Women's Experience of Sex, Sheila Kitzinger, Penguin Books, 1985

ORGANISATIONS AND CAMPAIGNS

Great Britain

Abortion Law Reform Association
88 Islington High Street
London N1
Tel: 01 359 5200

Birth Control Trust
27-35 Mortimer Street
London W1N 7RJ
Tel: 01 580 9360
Research and information on birth control, especially in relation to parliament and the law

Brook Advisory Centres
153a East Street
London SE17 2SD
Tel: 01 708 1234
Birth control advice and help for young people

Family Planning Association
27-35 Mortimer Street
London W1N 7RJ
Tel: 01 636 7866
Runs the Family Planning Information Service which gives information on all aspects of contraception including your local NHS family planning clinic details

British Pregnancy Advisory Service
Austy Manor
Wootton Wawan
Solihull
West Midlands
B95 6BX
Tel: 05642 3225
National headquarters, can put you in touch with nearest BPAS centre for advice on abortion, sterilisation and fertility problems

Copper 7 Association
28 Finlay Gardens
Addlestone
Weybridge
Surrey
KT19 2XN
Information and support for

those with bad experiences of
the Copper 7 IUD

Dalkon Shield Association
24 Patshull Road
London NW5
Co-ordinating legal cases against
the manufacturers of the Dalkon
Shield IUD as well as offering
information and support for
users

Health Education Council
78 New Oxford Street
London WC1A 1AH
Tel: 01 637 1881

**Scottish Health Education
Group**
Health Education Centre
Woodburn House
Canaan Lane
Edinburgh EH10 4SG
Tel: 031 447 8044
Both organisations provide
information leaflets on health
and fitness

The Herpes Association
39-41 North Road
London N7 9DP
Self-help group offering
information and support

Maternity Alliance
59-61 Camden High Street
London NW1 7JL
Tel: 01 388 6337
Campaigns for improved
services for mothers and
babies

Marie Stopes House
108 Whitfield Street
London W1
Tel: 01 388 4843
Services include abortion,
sterilisation, and reproductive
health

National Abortion Campaign
70 Great Queen Street
London WC2B 5AX
Tel: 01 405 4801
Campaigns to defend and extend
abortion rights

Natural Family Planning Unit
Birmingham Maternity Unit
Queen Elizabeth Medical Centre
Edgbaston
Birmingham 15
Information on fertility
awareness methods

Pregnancy Advisory Service
11-13 Charlotte Street
London W1
Tel: 01 637 8962
Advice and help on abortion,
sterilisation and reproductive
health for women living in
London and South East England

Sickle Cell Society
Willesden Hospital
Harlesden Road
Wood Green
London N22
Tel: 01 451 3293
Support and information for
those with sickle cell anaemia
and their families

Organisation for Sickle Cell Anaemia Research
22 Pellat Grove
Wood Green
London N22
Tel 01 899 4844

Terrence Higgins Trust
BM AIDS
WC1N 3XX
Tel: 01 278 8745
Advice and information on all aspects of Acquired Immune Deficiency Syndrome (AIDS) – has women counsellors and sub-group

Women's Health Information Centre
52-54 Featherstone Street
London EC1
Tel: 01 251 6580
Information on women's health – has register of groups and campaigns, and produces newsletter

Women's Reproductive Rights Information Centre
52-54 Featherstone Street
London EC1
Tel: 01 251 6332
Information on all aspects of contraception, abortion, sterilisation, reproductive health, infertility etc

Eire

Dublin:
Well Woman Centre
73 Lower Leeson Street
Dublin 2
Tel: 01 789511

Well Woman Centre
60 Eccles Street
Dublin 1
Tel: 01 728051

Irish Family Planning Association
5-7 Cathal Brugha Street
Dublin 1
Tel: 01 727276, 727363

Irish Family Planning Association
59 Synge Street
Dublin 8
(A Young People's Family Planning Centre is based at this address on Saturday afternoons between 1.00 and 5.00 p.m. The centre offers information, counselling and medical services especially for young adults.)
Tel: 01 682420, 780712

Family Planning Services
67 Pembroke Road
Dublin 8
Tel: 01 681108

Family Planning Services
78a Lower Georges Street
Dun Laoghaire

Co Dublin
Tel: 01 850666

**Adolescent Confidential
Telephone Service (ACTS)**
(Operates Saturday afternoons
between 1.00 and 5.00 p.m.
offering counselling and
information on relationships,
sexuality, conception,
contraception, VD and
pregnancy – run by young
people)
Tel: 01 740723, 744133,
729574

Out of Dublin:
Bray Family Planning Clinic
Dug Inn
Strand Road
Bray
Wicklow
Tel: 01 860410

Cork Family Planning Clinic
4 Tuckey Street
Grand Parade
Cork
Tel: 021 502906

**Galway Family Planning
Clinic**
Ryan Building
16 Merchants Road
Galway
Tel: 091 62992

**Limerick Family Planning
Clinic**
4 Mallow Street
Limerick
Tel: 061 312026

**Limerick Family Planning
Clinic**
14 South Quay
Newcastle West
Limerick

Tralee Family Planning Clinic
29 Rock Street
Tralee
Kerry
Tel: 066 25322

**Waterford Family Health
Centre Ltd**
7 Michael Street
Waterford
Tel: 051 78344

**Wexford Family Planning
Services**
16 Lower Georges Street
Wexford
Tel: 053 24638

*Help for Irish women coming to
Britain*
**Irish Women's Abortion
Support Group**
c/o Women's Reproductive
Rights Information Centre
(WRRIC)
52-54 Featherstone Street
London EC1Y 8RT
Tel: 01 251 6332

APPENDIX

Brand names of the pill in Australia and New Zealand

Combination pills containing 35-50 mcg of oestrogen:

Australia	New Zealand
Brevinor 21 & 28	Anovlar
Brevinor-1 21 & 28	Brevinor
Microgynon 50 & ED	Eugynon
Neogynon & ED	Gynovlar
Nordette 50	Lyndiol
Nordiol 21 & 28	Microgynon 50
Norinyl-1 21 & 28	Neogynon
Minovlar 21 & ED	Nordiol
Ortho-Novum 1/50	Norinyl-1
21 & 28	Norlestrin
Ovulen 0.5/50 & ED	Orlest
Ovulen 1/50 21 & 28	Ovostat
Minovlar 21 & ED	Ovral
	Ovulen 0.5
	Ovulen 1.0
	Ovulen 1/50
	Restovar

Combination pills containing 30 mcg or less of oestrogen:

Australia	New Zealand
Nordette 21 & 28	Marvelon
Microgynon 30 & ED	Nordette

Phased combination pills:

Australia	New Zealand
Biphasil	Biphasil
Sequilar ED	Synphasic
Synphasic	Triphasil
Triphasil	Triquilar
Triquilar & ED	

Progestogen only pills:

Australia	New Zealand
Microlut	Femulen
Micronor	Microlut
Microval	Microval
Noriday	Noriday

INDEX

Page numbers in *italic* refer to the illustrations